The Heart of Marketing

*Love Your Customers and
They Will Love You Back*

by

Judith Sherven, PhD & Jim Sniechowski, PhD

New York

The Heart of Marketing
Love Your Customers and They Will Love You Back

Copyright © 2009 Judith Sherven, PhD & Jim Sniechowski, PhD

Disclaimer: The Publisher and the Author make no representations or warranties with respect to the accuracy or completeness of the contents of this work and specifically disclaim all warranties, including without limitation warranties of fitness for a particular purpose. No warranty may be created or extended by sales or promotional materials. The advice and strategies contained herein may not be suitable for every situation. This work is sold with the understanding that the Publisher is not engaged in rendering legal, accounting, or other professional services. If professional assistance is required, the services of a competent professional person should be sought. Neither the Publisher nor the Author shall be liable for damages arising herefrom. The fact that an organization or website is referred to in this work as a citation and/or a potential source of further information does not mean that the Author or the Publisher endorses the information the organization or website may provide or recommendations it may make. Further, readers should be aware that internet websites listed in this work may have changed or disappeared between when this work was written and when it is read.

ISBN 978-1-60037-559-0

Library of Congress Control Number: 2008943939

MORGAN · JAMES
THE ENTREPRENEURIAL PUBLISHER

Morgan James Publishing, LLC
1225 Franklin Ave., STE 325
Garden City, NY 11530-1693
Toll Free 800-485-4943
www.MorganJamesPublishing.com

In an effort to support local communities, raise awareness and funds, Morgan James Publishing donates one percent of all book sales for the life of each book to Habitat for Humanity. Get involved today, visit **www.HelpHabitatForHumanity.org.**

Judith Sherven, PhD
&
Jim Sniechowski, PhD

Have you ever felt that still, small voice telling you there was something 'icky' about your marketing? Have you ever wished you could sell more of your products or services - and still be in alignment with your spiritual values? This book shows you how. Read it and be impressed. Put it into action, and be transformed.

> ~ Ray Edwards, Copywriter & Marketing Strategist,
> www.RayEdwards.com

When I read what Judith & Jim say about loving your customers I totally relate and connect with what they are saying. They've laid out the inner and outer magic of marketing with love in a way that every business owner should read and share with their staff members. When you love your customers and really care for them, your business will soar.

> ~ Christina Hills, The Shopping Cart Queen,
> www.ShoppingCartQueen.com

In *The Heart of Marketing* Judith and Jim give voice to powerful thoughts and concepts that many information marketers have been thinking and feeling for years. This book is an expression of the beginning of a movement that is changing the face of marketing as we have always known it. A new day is dawning, and I strongly urge you to get and use this book and come along.

> ~ Jeff Herring, The Article Marketing Guy,
> www.GreatArticleMarketingBlog.com

Relationship experts Judith & Jim have launched a new genre of marketing that takes the art of buying and selling and transforms it with the bond of love and trust.

> ~ Tracy Repchuk, best-selling author of
> *31 Days to Millionaire Marketing Miracles,*
> www.millionairemarketingmiracles.com

If your goal of selling your product or service is to truly help your customers, to love your customers, and to truly create value for them and for the world, then **you need this book**. But quite frankly, if your goal is anything else, then **you need this book more**!

~Mark Widawer, Internet Marketing Speaker, Educator,
www.MarkWidawer.com/heart-marketing-free-gift

We are in the midst of a great planetary awakening in our personal lives, as well as in our businesses. In this amazing book, Judith and Jim share their unique ability to articulate the need for morality, compassion, and oneness in the new world of Internet marketing. Their words of wisdom will help you to open and shape the way that you view your business, how you interact with others, and guide you down the path to a world of win/win for you and your clients.

~ Jody Colvard, CEO and Executive Producer,
www.FMGNetwork.com

Finally! It's about time a marketing book finally addressed one of the fundamental internal struggles many service professionals and purpose-driven entrepreneurs experience around marketing and selling. Transcending tricks and shortcuts *The Heart of Marketing* focuses on one of the cornerstones of building a massively successful business – understanding that great marketing is about falling in love with the people we serve through our work. But don't confuse it with idle theories; inside you will discover an amazingly practical guide to growing your business in the "new economy" and ideas you can use right away to turn loving your customers into bottom line profits!

~ Adam Urbanski, CEO of The Marketing Mentors,
www.TheMarketingMentors.com

Judith and Jim share their own business evolution in this groundbreaking book for the new millennia. You will discover not only step-by-step strategies to incorporate the selling is spiritual service mind-set into every one of your business's processes and systems, but how to activate this principle in your own soul. Get ready to LOVE doing business – because *that*, after all, *is the point*!

~ Baeth Davis, The Hand Analyst, www.handanalyst.com

One of the most powerful ways to sell is from the heart. This book is one of the best teaching tools I've seen around to do exactly that - It's a MUST read!

~ Matt Bacak, Internet Millionaire, www.promotingtips.com

Every author, healer, and spiritual person needs this book to bust through the myth that selling and spirituality are mutually exclusive. They are not. Thank you Judith and Jim.

~ Ellen Violette, The eBook Coach, www.theebookcoach.com

Judith and Jim put their energy and passion for marketing with heart into this book. Make sure to read it from cover to cover. Their vision and enthusiasm are contagious and they deliver results for their students.

~ Mike Filsaime, Internet Marketing Expert, www.MarketingDotCom.com

Judith & Jim let their love for soft sell marketing shine through. It's contagious! If you know in your heart that you are not a hard-sell type, this book is for you. If somewhere deep inside you know that your passion and love need an outlet, this book is for you.

~ Cathy Perkins, The Word Press Wizard, www.TheWordPressWizard.com

ABOUT TIME ... finally a book reveals the much needed quantum shift in 'selling technique' that will fundamentally transform the way you run your business forever.

> ~ Alan Forrest Smith, International Speaker, Consultant, Writer and Trainer, www.AlanForrestSmith.com

This is one fabulous read - deeply moving, inspiring, and a blueprint for the future of commerce offline and online.

> ~ Peggy McColl, best-selling author of
> *Your Destiny Switch,*
> www.peggymccoll.com

Reading this book is bound to have you saying "Amen!" It's such a breath of fresh air to have someone finally give a voice to the silent majority of people who have something to "sell". For most of us, "Selling" was something that didn't feel right to us. Sharing and being of service was more our style, and this book proves that we're not alone. I've spent the past 14 years working from home, sharing and helping people while making VERY nice money to boot. All I ever did was follow my heart and "do unto others". Judith and Jim have given you a plan to make that same dream come true for you too!

> ~ Frank Garon, America's Coast to Coast Internet Income Trainer, www.internetcashplanet.com

Coming from the relationships world where marketing (and business) is too-often seen as something icky, Judith and Jim had to reinvent the business world on their terms. The soft and ethical approach they developed is totally in keeping with the principles I've been advocating for years. As added bonuses, they write very well and effectively use their personal stories to bring their truths to light.

> ~ Shel Horowitz, award-winning author of
> *Principled Profit: Marketing That Puts People First,*
> www.business-ethics-pledge.org

I've been looking for some new ways to really connect with my customers on a deeper level. After reading *The Heart of Marketing* I've outlined 7 new ways to make my business more meaningful both to myself and my customers. All trends point to soft sell as the future for long-lasting, successful business. If you're not already on the boat you should be. This book is the boat!

> ~ Jae Jans, Editor-in-Chief, *Alchemist Magazine*,
> www.AlchemistMagazine.com

Designing my jewelry is second nature, selling it wasn't—until I read *The Heart of Marketing*. Now I see that selling really is a spiritual service. Thank you Judith & Jim for helping me pair my business goals with my spiritual commitment.

> ~ Bridget Gless, CEO, Bridget Gless Designs,
> www.bridgetglessdesigns.com

The Heart of Marketing is destined to become a marketing classic – it's that powerful! Using their years of insight into the psychology of message-to-market influence and persuasion, Judith & Jim show how to build intimacy-based sales relationships. They share **groundbreaking** tactics, strategies, and wisdom to accelerate rapid, repeated, and loyal buying behavior in a profoundly simple and direct way. It's exceedingly rare to find a book about sales psychology and influence that is this powerful!

> ~ Danny Guspie and Heidi Nabert, Co-Hosts of Divorced
> Dad Weekly, and Divorced DadMinute,
> www.DivorcedDadWeekly.com

An amazingly insightful, spiritually uplifting look at marketing. This book empowers you to promote your products and services by first and foremost promoting yourself. And it shows you how! What a rarity in the once-over-lightly world of typical book publishing.

> ~ Jill Lublin, best-selling author of *Get Noticed...Get Referrals*,
> www.JillLublin.com

Not everyone is a natural born salesperson, but we all need to sell in a competitive society in order to survive. Judith & Jim have provided a necessary roadmap for those who don't feel comfortable with the hard sell. This book is a must read for all sales people in these uncertain and competitive times.

~ Gary Goldberg, Gary Goldberg Financial Services, www.ggfs.com

The truly successful business on the Internet is one where the business owner invites you into their inner world, asks you what is important to you, and shows that they care. In *The Heart of Marketing* Judith and Jim have created a comprehensive and inspiring guide to this new way of doing business. It is an essential read if you are serious about creating a long lasting business.

~ Janet Beckers, Founder-Host, Wonderful Web Women, www.wonderfulwebwomen.com

What Judith and Jim have shared in this book is not just great wisdom for business, but practical, liberating advice that can be applied to pretty much any and every area of our lives. In a world full of so much hype, disillusionment and empty promises, this book will empower you to bypass the barriers that produce mediocre business results. Apply what this book teaches you and soon you will soar to the top of the hearts and minds of your customers, allowing you to love them with your gifts and have them loving you back with their wallets and praise!

~ Ruddy Ortiz, Info Marketing Specialist, www.TheInfoProfitSystem.com

This book is the bridge between soul, spirit, and sales. Others have addressed the issue, but Judith & Jim took the baton and have crossed the finish line with *The Heart of Marketing*.

~ Michelle Price, Chief Connectivity Officer, www.AThirdMind.com

Who would have ever imagined that words like heart, love, and spirit would so easily co-exist with selling and marketing? In this timely and insightful book, Judith and Jim reveal that they not only can co-exist, but that true business success ultimately depends on it. This must-read book replaces the often-held stigmas and stereotypes about sales and marketing with an inspiring new paradigm for business success based on integrity, connection, and meaning.

> ~ Lou D'Alo, Personal and Business Success Coach for
> Enlightened Entrepreneurs, www.PowerupCoaching.com

The Heart of Marketing proves that doing good and giving back pays off for everyone. Its wisdom confirms the way we work together can change business and, even more important, change the world. It proves the powerful connection between our spirit and the work we do. Read it, enjoy it, and experience authentic success.

> ~ Lori Prokop, Director of Social Media,
> Keyboard Culture New Earth Community™,
> www.keyboard-culture.com

A must read for professionals who did not grow up with the Internet, *The Heart of Marketing* explains the complex world of marketing in a way that anyone can understand. More important, it teaches professionals how to market themselves with dignity, so that they don't sound like a walking infomercial.

> ~ Glenn Shepard, President, Glenn Shepard Seminars,
> www.glennshepard.com

Judith and Jim offer a great big positive insight that will help every business owner right now! They deftly explain why selling with heart is essential to having a vibrant and healthy spiritual life. Not only do they explain it clearly, and in practical detail, they live the concept themselves, and the experience they share is something you can take to the bank. Bravo!

> ~ Diane A. Curran, Mozaique Media Arts,
> www.MozaiqueMediaArts.com

Judith and Jim's *The Heart of Marketing* reinforces the greater value you can offer potential clients, and shows how you only shortchange yourself and hurt your clients' progress when you hold back. This book gives you the knowledge and practical action tools to live in your fullest potential for the betterment of every life you get to touch.

> ~ Andy Duncan, Film Producer and Online Business Builder,
> www.andyduncan.name

Judith and Jim are masterful at relationships and this work is an extension of all their years of BEING the Love they talk about. They have made it comfortable for those of us who consider our work 'service' and who teach spiritual principles to see 'selling as a spiritual service'. I endorse this book wholeheartedly.

> ~ Rev. Dr. Toni La Motta, award-winning author of
> *What You REALLY Want, Wants You,*
> www.tonilamotta.com

Research has shown that great businesses are those that have "heart," as opposed to strictly left-brain, scientifically managed companies. "Relationship marketing" is the wave of the future. Ride the crest of the wave with Judith & Jim's new book *The Heart of Marketing*.

> ~ Dr. Andrew Colyer, Natural Health Expert,
> www.muscletestingtips.com

The Heart of Marketing is a powerful and moving read about the much needed shift in how we market our goods and services. Marketing is a multi-billion dollar business that has very little concern for the impact it has on the consumer. This book clearly shows how the shift toward heart in marketing should and must take place.

> ~ Diane McLain, Speaker, Coach, and Trainer,
> www.RemakeTheWorld.com

When it comes to books about marketing and selling, there are a lot of breakthrough titles, but few breakthrough books. Judith and Jim, have both in this wonderful guide to not only selling better but living better through their enlightening and profound process. Spiritual intention, from how to profit with their methods to application of their techniques, is life affirming and profit proving. They should know, it's what they do, not just what they preach.

> ~ Tom Justin, author of
> *How To Take No For An Answer and Still Succeed,*
> www.YourInnerWizard.com

Whether coaching or marketing, love is the most powerful influence, and this book shows you how to love your customers and gain financially - without guilt!

> ~ Terri Levine, author of best-selling *Coaching is for Everyone*,
> www.TerriLevine.com

As a real estate developer, people seldom imagine that I need to relate with customers, but Judith & Jim's book demonstrated how nearly everyone I work with is a customer. And now, thanks to *The Heart of Marketing*, I have a new perspective on the deeper connection we all share. It enhances my commitment to my work—and to all of my clients.

> ~ Paul Keller, Founder and Principal, Urban Partners,
> www.urbanpartnersllc.com

With every beat, our hearts create a frequency -- a vibration -- that touches the ends of the Universe connecting us to All That Is. This book, The Heart of Marketing, reveals the secret of that energy -- Love -- and teaches us to harness its sacred power and limitless possibility to touch the hearts of all who are hungry for what we offer.

> ~ Linda Pannell, Owner, Conscious Alliance,
> www.consciousalliances.com

We dedicate *The Heart of Marketing* to all soft sell marketers—
to each one of you, men and women around the globe,
who have committed your lives to making this world a better place
while also reaping the reward of money well-earned.

Contents

The real voyage of discovery consists not in seeking new landscapes, but in having new eyes.
Marcel Proust

Introduction

This book is about marketing. But more important, this is a book about you, the soft sell marketer, and your desire to market and sell your products and services online or off without compromising your values and what you believe about how people should be treated.

In short, it's about putting your heart into marketing.

As former therapists who ventured into online marketing just four years ago we had to overcome our technical deficiencies and learn to make friends with the computer. Even more so, we had to open our minds to an entirely new way of being in the world, a whole new and very different mindset—a marketing/business mindset.

We kept hearing from Internet marketing teachers about this strategy and that technique, and all we had to do was apply what we were learning and we would surely become successful Internet marketers. After all, they did, and, as they kept insisting—"You Can Too!!"

So we applied exactly what we were told, step-by-step, word-for-word—with some financial success. But all along we labored under the feeling that something was wrong. Or to put it more accurately, something just wasn't right. But what?

The answer began to emerge at the various Internet marketing conferences we attended.

We could hear that what the speakers were teaching was logical and credible. But we always felt a sense of displacement, a feeling of not belonging, of somehow being outsiders. We hadn't had years of business experience, no formal business education, and no family business connections. So we accepted our discomfort as just part of the newness we'd jumped into.

But at those same conferences we began to hear others who had the same complaint—"I don't feel right, somehow." We heard their complaints often enough that a pattern became clear. All those who voiced this kind of discomfort were service providers, care-givers, change agents of some kind, men and women who had dedicated their lives to helping others—heart-to-heart.

These people didn't have big money as their foremost objective. To be sure they all wanted to make money—a commensurate return for the value they provided. But equal to making money was their need to serve the well-being of their customers and clients, and in so doing, earn the income they desired—not the other way around.

They also expressed their resistance to and sometimes downright objection to competing and keeping score—i.e. making money for money's sake. And some uttered the word "selling" as though it were a profanity. It became clear that there was a segment of the Internet marketplace that was not being served. That segment is peopled by soft sell marketers—all of us who are care-givers and life-change artists as distinct from accumulation artists whose focus is money first and foremost.

If you relate to what we're saying, *The Heart of Marketing* is written to you and for you.

Several Objectives

We have several objectives that make up the overall intention of this book.

First, no competition: we make a clear distinction between soft sell marketing, which is emerging in the marketplace, and traditional hard sell marketing, a marketing style so common that it's assumed to be "natural" so most people take it for granted.

There is no competition between soft and hard sell. They are different and serve different customers. They each function from a different marketing mindset with different objectives. As we've just said:

> Soft sell marketers serve the well-being of their customers
> and clients as their primary objective, and in so doing earn
> the income they desire—not the other way around.

Hard sell marketing focuses on money first and foremost and, in so doing serves its customers— not the other way around.

Second, heart-based: we validate and support the value of the heart-to-heart connections brought to the marketplace by soft sell marketers. Their need for a felt connection between seller and buyer creates a level of emotional authenticity and transparency that adds a dimension to a sale beyond a mere commercial transaction.

Even on the Internet, where a customer may be on the other side of the world, the soft sell need for connection is expressed through the intent to create a relationship as the basis for the commercial transaction.

Third, commercially successful: we present the principle that Selling Is Spiritual Service with the intent to heal the split that soft sell marketers feel between their desire to be of service and their need to be paid, and paid well for what they do. Care-givers, whose lives are grounded in heart-to-heart connections, have historically been viewed as those who should work without ambition for money, because it was thought that money would corrupt the value of tending to those in need.

We repudiate that notion and point to the validity and social value inherent in soft sell marketers' ambitions to generate money as it ranks second but equal to their concern for the well-being of their customers and clients.

Finally, spiritually rewarding: it's our aim to provide support for and articulate the internal aspects of marketing, because a successful sale is more than just numbers and product delivery. Every successful sale, whether soft sell or hard sell, is a co-creation of both the buyer and the seller, regardless of whether either or both are aware of their fundamental interdependence.

Quoting John Muir, naturalist and founder of the Sierra Club—"When we try to pick out anything by itself, we find it hitched to everything else in the Universe."

The interconnectedness in which we all live is the signature statement of Creation. So it does all of us well, financially and spiritually, to keep aware of this undeniable fact. And when we do, we market through a broader lens of consciousness and a deeper sense of conscience.

That's why our objective is to open and inspire your soft sell imagination and set a foundation for your understanding and use of soft sell marketing.

772 Questions

The Heart of Marketing is based on an online survey we took while promoting our second "Bridging Heart and Marketing" Internet marketing conference which was held in September, 2008. We simply asked—

What Do You Most Want To Know About Soft Sell Marketing?

We received 772 questions from respondents all over the world. Their questions were split between external, tactical requests—"Where to begin?"— and internal, mindset requests—"How do I resolve the emotional conflict between my desire to serve and my desire for money?"

We've chosen 45 questions that best represent the key concerns expressed by those who answered our survey, and they form the basis for this book.

In answering these questions we begin with "What is marketing?" and "Who are soft sell marketers?" and end with "Do you see soft sell marketing as a trend in the future?"

We welcome you to the new world of heart-based, soft-sell marketing, and trust that it will inspire deeper and richer connections with your customers and more enjoyment and fulfillment in your business life.

From Therapists To Marketers

During the Fall of 2001, for reasons we'll make clear in a bit, we were living in Windham, a small mountain town in upstate New York (population 1600), virtually unemployed and looking for a way to generate income.

We'd given up successful psychotherapy practices in Santa Monica and moved to New York in 2000 hosting our own radio show for Wisdom Radio with the strong possibility, as we were told, that we would be taken on by WOR in Manhattan, one of the major stations in the country. They wanted a socially conscious show and, as best selling authors and very media savvy, we were exactly what they were looking for.

Well paid for our Wisdom Radio show, all we needed was to wait for the call from WOR.

Windham was blissful. Beautiful and serene. Deer and wild turkey, geese and wild blackberries in our back yard. People in town welcomed us and we never looked back.

Rural life gave us the quiet we needed to finish writing our third book, *Be Loved for Who You Really Are,* and we had the time and money to do whatever we otherwise wanted.

We'd been told that a good way to jump start book sales was to publish an online ezine. So, in preparation for the release of *Be Loved*, we started a weekly relationship ezine and it wasn't long before we'd built our list to 35,000 subscribers.

Can you just see it? Our future? WOR and a spot on the New York Times best seller list!?

Could things have been better?

An Unconscious Flaw

To reveal the flaw in this picture we have to go back to our first book, *The New Intimacy*, published in 1997 by Health Communications, Inc. We had received very positive reviews and the book sold well given that we were first-time authors.

However, wanting *The New Intimacy* to sell to an even larger audience, as large an audience as possible, we ventured far beyond the art of counseling into the gutty world of business.

Our publicist for *The New Intimacy* told us—"Give me a good title and cover, a good first chapter and a good last chapter. I don't care what you put in the middle."

We thought she was joking. She wasn't. She understood marketing and selling.

We were therapy artists and writers. We had no background in business. None. Zero.

Our therapy practice was precisely that—a practice—all based on quality work and referrals. We never had to market. We never had to sell. We never had to make persuasive presentations. Our therapeutic work stood on its own and sold us better than we ever could have ourselves.

But having jumped into the world of book selling, we organized and scheduled, on our own, hundreds of radio and television appearances as well as 89 book signings for *The New Intimacy* at bookstores around the country. The net result, however, was largely publicity. We had no idea that the purpose of marketing was to lay out the problems people faced and strongly make the point that our book was the solution. In other words—prepare our customers to buy.

We didn't do that because we didn't know to do it. Believing what we were doing was the best approach, we gave away a lot of information, limiting the number of books sold.

> **Judith:** For example, we made a presentation at one of the best bookstores in Los Angeles and we invited a dear friend to attend. After the event she told us that when she was in the ladies room she overheard a woman telling a friend, "I

don't need to buy their book. They laid it all out during their talk."

Jim: We were so committed to our belief that it was solely the quality of the book that should make the sale that we repeatedly and unwittingly limited book sales by giving away the content.

The book business is a business. Clear and simple. It's all about marketing and selling. And we suffered the fatal flaw of being unschooled in business and marketing. Coupled with an unbounded idealism—which might be called "fantasyism"—we were as naive as they come.

While *The New Intimacy* made it onto the Los Angeles Times Best Seller List, we were frustrated with the book not becoming a huge hit. Yet we didn't know what else to do but keep forging ahead. So we did.

Fate Stepped In and On Us

Now fast forward to 2001. Our third book, *Be Loved for Who You Really Are*, was ready. Under contract to a substantial publisher and with an online list of 35,000, we were filled with anticipation for *Be Loved* to be released in late October, 2001.

But the attack on the World Trade Center in September 2001 rocked our world, as it did everyone else's. Suddenly, learning to be loved for who you really are couldn't have been more irrelevant in the eyes of the media when measured against the physical and psychological assault we all experienced that September 11th.

So our book, our beautiful and very wise book, was thrust into the horrors of war and orphaned to a life of near invisibility.

Then, from bad to worse, in December of 2001 we parted ways with Wisdom Radio.

Judith: Their idea of "Spiritual Programming" became a relentless demand that we deliver our show in a virtual whisper—what they believed the voice of reverence and spirituality was supposed to sound like.

Their producers complained that we "played too much," that my laugh was "too loud."

Jim: They said that I cared too much about social and cultural issues instead of the inner dynamics of a spiritual relationship.

They never said it in words but what they meant was that we were selling out to typical commercial radio and not adhering to their "high" spiritual standards.

It became just too painful on both sides so we parted company—which left us virtually unemployed by January 2002—in a small town of 1600—a position neither of us had ever experienced before.

A Turning Point in Our Soft Sell History

In the Fall of 2004, after nearly three years scrambling to pay our bills, researching and writing our fourth book, *The Smart Couple's Guide to the Wedding of Your Dreams,* writing several screenplays, and working on various other projects, we were more than ready for something that would open us to a larger future.

One evening Judith listened to a teleseminar in which Alex Mandossian was promoting his first-time tele-course, "Teleseminar Secrets." The call hadn't ended before Judith knew we had to take it. She saw it as a way we could generate a substantial income.

Alex's "Teleseminar Secrets" course was our first conscious step into the world of marketing. Alex rightfully taught that taking action was the only way to learn. So, as the course progressed, he encouraged everyone to give their own teleseminars.

Eager students, experienced speakers and workshop leaders, we didn't hesitate to give our first couple of free teleseminars: "Keeping Romance Alive," which became the basis for one of our most popular relationship products, and "The Promise of Conflict," which is a staple in our line of products.

To market our teleseminars, he told us to write an announcement about what we would be teaching in our teleseminar, describe some of the benefits, and invite people to register. We sent that announcement to the people we'd met at book signings and elsewhere, whose email addresses were kept in Judith's AOL address book.

We followed exactly what Alex told us to do and produced two successful teleseminars.

Then, with two successes behind us, we decided it was time to charge for our service.

We put together a tele-course, "Smart Dating for Success Every Time – Guaranteed!" from the material we'd been teaching for years. We would give it on two successive Wednesdays, each call consisting of two hours of material followed by thirty minutes of Q & A, for a total of five hours.

But . . . we had no idea what to charge.

So, during a Q & A session we asked Alex for his advice on pricing. When he heard the topic was dating, even though the course would be four hours of content and an hour of Q & A, he said, "Ohhh, hmmmm, that's a soft topic. You're not going to get much for that. I think you could maybe get $19.95."

> **Judith:** For five hours of our hard won, already tested and proven relationship wisdom! ONLY $19.95! No Way!!

> **Jim:** Talk about puncturing the heart of our excitement!

We were horrified. But, with regard to Internet pricing, we were also insecure. Refusing Alex's suggestion, we priced our first course at $47.

We booked 28 students, all personal contacts, again from our list stored in Judith's AOL address book—taking their orders via email and phone, because we didn't yet have a shopping cart.

The course was a smash hit, resulting in many unsolicited, glowing testimonials.

When we reported our success to Alex he was amazed.

So we grew bolder.

Following what Alex taught, we created a Joint Venture with friends who owned Transitions Bookplace, a major bookstore in Chicago. We sent email notices to their list and had 187 people on the line for our free preview call. We booked 17 for the two-week course, this time with a tuition of $75 per person.

Alex was truly impressed—both with the price and that our conversion rate was almost ten percent.

Still not sure of the real price-point for the course, we taught it again. This time, however, we called it "The Smart Dating Summit." As bonuses, we included a CD of "Keeping Romance Alive" and copies of all of our books, and we priced it at $247. We had nine grateful students.

Alex was dumbfounded.

> **Judith:** We had our first glimpse into the black hole prevelant in traditional thinking about so-called soft topic info-marketing . . .

> **Jim:** And we saw there was a huge gap in the traditional online marketplace that had not been identified and was certainly not being served.

Please understand, our successes were pretty much hit-and-miss, because we had no instincts for business. We were lucky and we enjoyed the hits. But everything we learned, every success we won, we won one step at a time. We're not complaining, but it was a grueling education.

Another Unanticipated Door Opened

Soon after Alex's course ended, we set up an affiliate teach-and-promote call to interview Alex and promote the hard copy version of Teleseminar Secrets (which he doesn't produce anymore). We invited our list and Alex promoted the call to those on his list who hadn't taken the course.

Not only did we make several sales and receive a tasty affiliate check, during the call Alex suddenly announced that everyone who ordered the course that night would receive an additional bonus. They would get a one-year "Teleseminar Secrets Coaching Program" with us—Judith & Jim—two hours per month for 12 months.

We were pop-eyed as we stared across the desk at each other. Alex had never asked if we'd be willing to do such a thing *and* we'd just taken his course so we were sheer newbies ourselves. But what were we going to say, "Uh . . . no, Alex, we're going to decline?"

Suddenly we were Teleseminar Secrets coaches, thrown into the deep end of the pool. What were we going to do?

Well, we're both PhDs and studying was one skill we'd perfected. So study we did. And the richest bonus to us from this unexpected and fortuitous command performance was our need to study the course more thoroughly and remain one step ahead of our students.

Jim was the study leader, and, during his intense immersion into the course, he made two career-changing discoveries.

He quickly realized, even more deeply than during the course itself, that much of the Internet marketing lingo Alex used was incomprehensible to people like us—former therapists who had no tech or business skills.

So Jim created a 25-page "Teleseminar Secrets Internet Marketing Glossary" defining, explaining, and elaborating all the terms in Alex's material we didn't understand. And we're proud to say that Alex uses it to this day as a bonus for his course.

Even more important was our growing awareness that like most caregivers—as compared with business people—we both carried a strong aversion to the idea of selling.

> **Judith:** I associated selling with hype and groveling desperation.

> **Jim:** I saw it as a disguised form of combat.

But we couldn't deny that at the very heart of any business is the need to sell. No selling, no business, no money. And it was no less true on the Internet.

So how were we going to coach our students about the need to sell? If they were like us, they too lived with an aversion, at least, or a repulsion at worst, to the whole idea of selling.

Jim: I set about meditating on the problem of selling and had one of those AHA's that changes your life forever. I saw that . . .

If there's someone out in the world with a problem they can't solve . . .

And you have a genuine solution that would bring relief and value into their life . . .

You have an ethical, moral, and spiritual obligation to market your product or service so that those who need you can find you.

If you don't, you shortchange yourself, you shortchange those who need what you offer, and you shortchange whatever you believe The Highest Power to be. In other words, when understood deeply—selling is spiritual service.

Viewing the selling process as heart-based, spiritual service was one of the most liberating, empowering, and inspiring moments of our young marketing career. It was our first wholly conscious step toward the vision and work we do today—"Bridging Heart and Marketing," the Internet marketing conference we produce; the Soft Sell Marketers Association which is dedicated to providing support and learning for soft sell marketers; and this book, *The Heart of Marketing*.

Yet Another Door Opened

After teaching "Smart Dating" live a number of times, recording the calls and having the recordings transcribed, we decided to package it into a home study course. This was a major step because it required conscious, professional marketing—a sales page and sales copy.

Even though we were writers, we had never given any thought to writing sales copy. So we worked with a very reputable, experienced, and accomplished copywriter. He was a terrific guy and we liked him very much.

He reviewed the program along with our books, talked with us at length about what we wanted, and we thought he really understood the need for heart-based, relationship-oriented sales copy.

> **Judith:** After all, "Smart Dating" is dedicated to the more conscious and mature man or woman who is ready to be in a serious, committed relationship.

> **Jim:** He said he understood, and more so, could feel the tone and voice needed to appeal to our specific audience.

Then, after several weeks, he returned a sales letter with the following headline:

"YOU'RE DOING SOMETHING ALL WEEK LONG THAT'S SCREWING UP YOUR SEX LIFE ON SATURDAY NIGHT, AND YOU DON'T EVEN KNOW WHAT IT IS!"

What? No way!! Totally unacceptable.

What were we to do?

We worked to see if we could lead him toward what we wanted, but to no avail. It became eminently clear that if we were going to get the feel and voice we wanted we'd better write our own sales copy.

After all, we were best-selling authors. Why not? So we did.

And, very much to our surprise, Alex Mandossian told us, "I keep a file of your copywriting. It's that good." And he suggested we teach what we were doing because no one else was. He even gave us the name for the course—"Soft Topic Copywriting Secrets."

So we did.

Our "Soft Topic Copywriting Secrets" course was an immediate success and put us in close touch with a wide variety of soft sell marketers—for example an ADHD medical doctor, interior decorator, anger management specialist, women's chorale producer, alternative oncologist, home schooling resource consultant, sexual enhancement expert, and a wide range of other specialists including a broad range of coaches and healers—almost all of them with a strong spiritual underpinning to their work.

While we taught the next group, and then the next—and as we attended a wide variety of Internet conferences and trainings—we came to the riveting, career changing conclusion that there needed to be a way for what we now call the soft sell community to get the specific kind of training and support they needed to create an authentically heart-based, commercially successful, and spiritually rewarding presence on the web.

> **Judith:** From that vision our widely acclaimed and popular "Bridging Heart and Marketing" conferences were born.

> **Jim:** We decided to bring together leading experts in Internet marketing who we experienced as heart-felt in the way they conducted their businesses . . .

> **Judith:** And because we rarely saw even a single woman speaker at any of the many Internet conferences we'd attended, we determined that on our stage the balance would be 50/50—which we have accomplished and will continue to do so.

Our events not only offer leading edge Internet marketing information, they change people's lives deeply—testified by the growing list of unsolicited emails we receive from attendees—because our events fill that gap in the marketplace where service providers and care-givers live.

It's Much, Much Larger than Business-to-Business

The fact is that the soft sell marketing community is much larger than the business-to-business, marketer-to-marketers group.

But when you're dedicated to helping people change their lives, dedicated to helping the world become sustainable, helping consciousness expand in order to advance our presence on this planet, it's unlikely that you have a business degree, unlikely that you studied finance, economics, or marketing, and it's even unlikely that you are comfortable commanding fees that represent your expertise and the value you bring to this world.

Yet, the world is sorely in need of the vision and heart exemplified by the soft sell community:

> **Judith:** That's why our work in support of our community—the soft sell community—is so important to us.

> **Jim:** And that's why we created the Soft Sell Marketers Association (SSMA) to provide ongoing training, community support, and marketing fun!

> **Judith:** We're very proud that SSMA is a worldwide gathering place for this amazing community of heart-based, spiritually motivated care-givers—especially at this time when the world is in such need of care and healing. (http://www.softsellmarketersassociation.org)

Changing the Face of the Marketplace

Beyond the mindset of hard sell marketing that often uses combat-style sales copy language like—

"Killer Copy"

"Insane Profits"

"Crush Your Competition" . . .

there lies a field of dreams—the dreams of every marketer who truly cares about the well-being of their customers, where respect and concern for themselves and their customers ranks equally with their desire for profits. And it is these marketers who are changing the face of sales, one heart-based sale at a time, one spiritually inspired marketing campaign at a time.

It's these marketers who are changing the way more and more people think about their business—whether or not it's on the Internet.

If If you are one of them, *The Heart of Marketing* is intended for you!

Because each time you step forward to advance how we marketers think and feel about customers, about business, about sales, about making money, you contribute to changing the world psyche. You move the pendulum just a bit further in the direction of interdependence, mutual protection, and ultimately mutual trust.

Not only do you advance the reputation of selling, you advance civilization. And that is the power of marketing and sales—the power we all have as we conduct heart-based commerce each and every day.

In that vision we want to see you succeed beyond what you now can even imagine, and that's why we support the growth and expansion of your marketing platform.

To that end we created our program "How To Grow Your Soft Sell Marketing Platform," and it's our gift to you.

Just go to:
http://www.bridgingheartandmarketing.com/platformbonus

Why Does Selling Have Such A Bad Reputation?

It's remarkable that sales and marketing have such a bad reputation. After all, with millions of men and women around the world directly involved in sales, you'd think it would be one of our most revered professions.

But it isn't.

So before we provide an in-depth and persuasive view of the financial and spiritual value of soft sell marketing, it's important that we uproot and clarify the reasons that selling suffers from such an undermining reputation.

When you think about it, it's actually mind boggling that an activity as basic as selling—"I will give you this if you give me that"—is so deeply mistrusted and maligned. It's almost as though humans discovered that oxygen can be dangerous, so we do our best not to breathe. But breathe we must.

And the same goes for selling. We can't get by without selling. Commerce is one of the basic languages we use to conduct our lives. Every day you enter into some type of sales process to insure that you have the necessities you need to stay alive. It's unavoidable. That's why we say that selling really is as basic as breathing.

A Different Style of Selling

On the corner of a major intersection near us a man appears almost every day dressed in a different costume. Once he's Darth Vader, then a rock star. Next he's a soldier in fatigues and then an Egyptian Pharaoh.

We've been living in Las Vegas for 18 months and we've never seen him dressed the same way twice.

We have no idea where he gets his outfits or how he pays for them. And he's clearly not in the same mental state most of the rest of us inhabit.

Still, he's out there for a couple of hours most every day waving at traffic, blowing kisses to the drivers, kneeling and praying (at least that's what it looks like), bending over and pointing at his butt, singing, shouting, expressing whatever is going on in his world.

In fact it's a letdown when he's not there.

So what's the point? The point is . . .

He's selling: I will give you this if you give me that. He puts on his performance to get our attention. And we buy. We give him our attention every time.

Even this man, in his world, can't get by without selling.

Why This Story?

Because we are selling. We consciously chose to open this chapter with three selling techniques to catch your attention. Our goal is to engage your imagination and draw you further into this book with:

- A Hook—"Why Does Selling Have Such A Bad Reputation?"—a provocative question, and questions are natural hooks. Our brain demands an answer;

- A Story—Stories are the best selling tools available. Stories capture the imagination. You begin to picture the event and become a co-creator in the project;

- And A Call To Action—when we said, "Even this man, in his world, can't get by without selling," we were implicitly asking for the order—in this case, your agreement.

So we were and are selling. We will give you the information in this book if you will give us your time and attention. An exchange of value for value.

What Is Selling?

So that we all start from the same understanding, let's be clear about what selling is at its root. It's an exchange. You provide a solution to the buyer's problem or desire in exchange for a commensurate return in the form of money. That's it. Simple.

As the buyer you have a problem you can't solve, large or small, or a desire you can't fulfill and you go looking for someone or something to provide what you need. That someone is the seller and that something is his/her solution to your need or desire.

When selling is done well, with integrity and a sincere intent to serve the needs of the buyer, you, as the seller, love your customers. Then this transaction is the beginning of a long lasting, mutually beneficial commercial (and maybe even personal) relationship. In this way your customers love you back.

For Example

We are best-selling authors of four books published by traditional publishing companies. But we became dissatisfied with that process and, when we knew we wanted to write this book, we had the challenge and opportunity of finding a different kind of publisher.

We didn't want to self-publish. So we researched our options until we discovered Morgan James, the publisher of this book. Their approach gave us the best of traditional publishing along with an entrepreneurial freedom that has made working with them a joy.

We offered them value—this book—and they offered us value—their publishing and distribution expertise. Both sides of the transaction were selling to and buying from each other. And we both treated each other with respect, integrity, and a depth of care. Problem solved. Relationship opened.

Yet Selling Still Takes the Wrap

We all live with problems to be solved and desires we want fulfilled, and bottom line—this can't be accomplished without marketing and selling. Yet it's selling, both the idea and the practice, that takes the wrap. People suspect and badmouth it.

Many people have shared with us that no matter how successful they become they can hear that old mind chatter, what we call Negative Head Talk, working away, trying to discredit and undermine what they're doing. They know it goes back to old, ingrained beliefs about selling as wrong, pushy, manipulative, greedy, and crass. They're still burdened with what keeps them stuck in place.

One man said, "Even though I've come a long way, that bewitching, almost inaudible negative voice is still there."

Are You Resistant to Being Sold?

It's taken as common sense that "People love to buy. They just hate being sold."

When you are the buyer, aren't you resistant to "being sold"—you know—maneuvered, snookered, taken for a ride, sweet-talked, hornswaggled, pushed around, scammed, ripped off, or just plain talked into it? If that is what's going on, then you have every reason to be repulsed by someone who is just trying to fleece your wallet.

Yet, even though most sellers are honorable people, working to help you make a wise decision while they also make a living, we are all so suspicious of being sold that we become trapped in our own imaginings.

When you are the seller, though your intentions are clear and clean, you still get lumped in with the snake oil salesman—even in your own mind. You're struggling uphill with an invisible granite block of guilt on your back as you work, hope, and pray to overcome your tangle of conflicting intentions.

This internal knot is particularly true for service providers and care-givers who are especially burdened by the belief that there's something wrong with selling.

In fact, we've been told by a number of people that "If I didn't have to sell I wouldn't. But how else do I make money?"

How Did We All Come to Cast Such a Pall Over Selling?

Recently we upgraded our computers. Jim will take the story from here.

> **Jim:** It was my job to research what we needed and choose where we were going to buy. I checked out a number of stores and the sales guy, Mike, at Best Buy really impressed me.
>
> He answered all of my questions, thoroughly and patiently—I'm not a computer whiz so I asked a lot of questions—even though I told him I wasn't ready to make the buy. Later I told Judith how comfortable I felt with him because he really cared.
>
> I then scheduled an appointment so we would be sure to work with him for the purchase, and told him I was going to take the SONY "VAIO" I'd looked at.
>
> Now here's what happened the day we bought.
>
> As we drove to the store Judith and I were chatting, excited about the upgrade. I was proud of my research. I knew what I wanted and knew what I wanted to pay. We could afford it.
>
> Then, as we were walking from the car to the store our pleasure at what was about to happen grew because we were looking forward to the new computer. Life was good.
>
> But as I stepped into the store, an emotional darkness rose up inside me. It was palpable. A startling contrast to how I'd felt just on the other side of the door.
>
> I didn't say anything to Judith because I wanted to observe this bizarre emotional shift. I felt like I was in danger. "I had damn sure better not let my guard down," I thought. I felt like I'd entered a den of predators where I was the only prey.

Fortunately I still had enough of myself intact to watch this amazing upsurge overtake me, and, as best as I could rationally tell, there was no good reason for it. Yet I was filled with it. Literally. A sense of dread.

As we approached the computer section Mike saw me and smiled. He seemed happy to see me. And why not? We'd enjoyed each other the day he was so helpful, and we had an appointment. He knew a sale was about to be made.

But the best I could do was think that he only *seemed* to be happy to see me. I couldn't find in me the possibility that he *actually was* happy to see me.

I was like Dr. Jekyll and Mr. Hyde.

"Hi, Jim," he smiled. "Ready to do it?"

I'd fallen into the night of the zombies. His smile suddenly looked like a sneer—like someone who knows he's about to do you in, and knows there's nothing you can do to stop him, and he can't wait to get started.

I realize that this sounds like I should have been in a psychiatric lock-up ward rather than Best Buy, but I was acutely aware of what was going on in me and wanted to watch.

Judith and I had already begun our adventure as Internet marketers and we'd talked about why people felt such a resistance to the selling process, so I was my own personal laboratory, experiencing resistance in spades.

Mike pointed to the desktop display and led the way. He was heading straight for the SONY.

As we passed the other desktops I heard myself thinking, "What about that one? Maybe that's a better choice. Why didn't he tell me about that one?"

At the SONY display I told Judith why I'd decided on that model. I didn't have to explain myself because first, she wasn't then very computer literate, and second, she trusted me.

As I was giving reasons for my choice, I kept hearing that voice in my head mutter, "You don't know what you're talking about. That was stupid. Look at Mike, he knows. He sees you."

I didn't actually hear a voice. It was more like a feeling. But it was merciless.

All the while the rebellious part of me kept saying, "What's going on here? What am I doing? I don't have to buy the thing. I can just walk out."

"Oh yeah," another side shot back, "That's great. Walk out. That'll impress everybody. Go ahead. Just leave." My internal drama went on for about ten minutes while we were all talking.

Finally Mike said, "Is this the one you want?" And I said, "Yes." Suddenly the darkness vanished as instantly as it appeared. I was free to enjoy what was left of the process.

What happened?

The Source of Our Resistance

Judith and I had been thinking a lot about resistance during the selling/buying process and wanted to understand it better, hopefully to its core. And my computer buying experience couldn't have been clearer evidence of what we'd been looking for.

After all, what's business all about? Making money, right? Short and simple. $$$.

Business and bucks. They're spelled differently but mean the same thing.

That's what everybody believes, right? That's just the way it is.

Now and then there might be genuine care involved, like with Mike. But when push comes to shove, care takes a back seat to the bottom line.

Cash is the default measure of value. On both sides. How much the seller can get or how little the buyer has to spend. That's the silent assumption that precedes the sale.

So what's the big deal? Why do people resist the sales process?

Because, for all of our protests and hopes to the contrary, traditionally business has not been about human emotional connection—the heart-to-heart connection. It's about $$$. Short and simple.

And it's just that lack of emotional connection that is the source of our resistance.

Both sides—seller and buyer—are reduced to objects in service to the numbers. Both sides, disempowered as people, dutifully play out their roles as cogs in what is called "the marketplace."

The problem is we are all objectified.

Objectification makes the transaction mechanical—riddled with marketing and sales techniques instead of sincere interest and connection. Each side becomes a mere functionary in the other's money game.

Then we become objects to be maneuvered instead of people to be served. Unconsciously, if not consciously, we can sense the danger. Who you are, how you feel, and what you want is reduced to how much money will change hands.

Is it any wonder that we resist?

So Where Do We Go From Here?

The answer to this question serves as the guide for the rest of this book. Because *The Heart of Marketing* is about loving your customers—about the very real and sincere emotional connection that can change the face and feel of commerce for everyone's benefit.

It's about infusing sincere, non-manipulative emotional connection into our commercial systems—locally and globally. Because the world at large suffers from the impact of business as a strictly numbers game—a game founded on calculation instead of connection.

We know you may argue—"That's crazy. You can't get emotional and run a successful business."

But, we ask, "Why not?" Where is it written that emotions and business do not mix—except as a culturally accepted habit elevated to the status of an eternal principle?

Maybe you're thinking—"There's plenty of emotion in business."

Yes, but what kind?

Emotion that celebrates goal achievement?
Emotion that praises financial growth?
Emotion that trumpets competitive domination?
Emotion at a distance.

What about intimate emotion?
Tender emotion?
Emotion up close?
The emotion of caring.

What about caring for the well being of those who will use your products and services, caring for their humanity in addition to their payment? What would it be like if that kind of caring lived at the core of the way we all do business? What would it be like if instead of closing the sale you opened the relationship? What would our business world look like if genuine connection was at the heart of marketing? At the heart of our political world? At the heart of our personal world?

We've written *The Heart of Marketing* as an invitation to think about selling in a new light:

- Selling with consciousness and conscience;

- Selling with caring and connection;

- Selling that makes what goes on in the marketplace an exchange of value, to be sure. But also an exchange of awareness that we are all interdependent upon one another.

We all need each other. And in that need—that existential and spiritual need—we would do well to treat each other with consciousness and conscience, aware that what we do and how we do what we do has impact. Not a trivial, topical impact. Not just dollars and cents. But an appreciation and respect for both the buyer and seller's hope and meaning in the exchange, for the need and desire that is alive on both sides of a transaction.

The Heart of Marketing is dedicated to the changes in your business and in your life when you recast the process of selling to acknowledge it for the indispensable human activity that it is, and then grant it a status that reflects the depth of its material, personal, and yes, its true spiritual value.

****

To understand The Power and Profit of Soft Sell Marketing, be sure to download your free copy of our 60-minute MP3 audio at http://tinyurl.com/sspbonus

45 Questions Answered

We're thankful to each of the 772 people who responded to our survey on soft sell marketing and generously sent in their questions.
What follows are the 45 questions we selected to answer, expressing the dominant concerns of soft sell marketers.

To gain the most benefit from the questions and answers that follow, and to make reading this book deeply personal, pay attention to how they apply to you and your business.

To tap the force of the universe itself,
we must see ourselves as part of the world
rather than separate from it.
Gregg Braden

#1. This may sound way too simple, but what is marketing?

This question is not at all too simple. In fact it's the very question that must be answered to create a solid foundation for your business.

We've been involved in Internet marketing for four years and to date no one has ever given us a solid definition of what marketing actually is.

Typically people describe marketing as "making yourself known in the marketplace" or "occupying space in the consumer's mind." These descriptions are correct but they don't provide a solid framework that takes you from the beginning to the end of a marketing campaign and leads to successful sales. Why? Because they don't tell you what to do once you are known in the marketplace or when you occupy a space in the consumer's mind.

So, to be clear about the actions you take when designing your marketing campaigns and the specific purpose of those actions, as well as all the details within each campaign, here's a perspective that will help ensure your efforts will be productive.

Preparing Your Customer to Buy

The essence of selling is converting your prospective customer into an actual customer. And the essence of marketing is—preparing your prospective customer to buy.

When you post something on your blog, or comment on someone else's blog, what's your purpose? When you hand out a business card, what's your purpose? When you enter a tweet on Twitter, or put up a page on Facebook, what's your purpose?

To make yourself known in the marketplace? Sure. To burrow your way into the customer's mind? Perhaps. But once you're in the marketplace or have a spot in the reader's mind what's your purpose for being there? Once you look at it this way it becomes obvious. You're there because you want your prospective customer to buy from you.

We are not saying that all you do is send out an endless array of sales pitches. That would be understanding our definition of marketing—preparing your customer to buy—as a tactic. No. "Preparing your customer to buy" is an underlying principle and needs to be your intention—present at all times—in everything you do as a marketer.

For example, the purpose of one of your blog posts may be to simply present an idea. But aren't you putting forward your message to seek a response from your readers? By seeking their response aren't you asking your readers to take an action with regard to what you say—either agreeing or not? That's not a cash sale, but it certainly is "I'll give you this if you'll give me that."

The same applies the first time you give someone your business card. Why bother if you don't eventually want to do something with that person? So you introduce yourself. And you announce, through your card, who you are and what you do as a way of preparing the other person to buy into the possibility of some future involvement with you.

During one of our weekly training calls for the members of our Soft Sell Marketers Association we focused on the idea of preparing your customer to buy. We noticed that one of the men was interpreting the word "buy" in an immediate sense—meaning an exchange of money. But that makes marketing a very driven, everything-on-the-line-right-now process, and that's not what we mean.

Know, Like, and Trust You

Instead, marketing is the process of taking your customer along a particular path at the end of which is an anticipated sale. But that sale is usually not immediate. It takes between three to nine impressions before someone does buy, so all you can do is prepare the way so that your potential customer grows to know you, like you, and trust you. That's what you're doing when you're making yourself known in the marketplace and when you're occupying a space in your customer's mind. Preparing them to buy your product or service when they are ready.

In other words, you are creating a relationship. The ultimate sale is your intention, and that's why your efforts, however subtle, are aimed at preparing your potential customer to buy. It's the relationship you've created and sustained that supports and advances the path to the sale.

So you are doing both. You are creating the relationship as you prepare your prospective customer to buy. And you do that for the well-being of both you and your customer—as we will show you throughout the rest of this book.

Without understanding this essential point your marketing efforts will likely be very frustrating. Why? Because you won't specifically know what you are doing and won't be able to communicate clearly and effectively. No matter how much effort you put out, your intentions will be misdirected.

A Perfect Example

When we lived in Los Angeles we produced a weekend seminar called "The Magic of Differences: The Source of the Deepest Intimacy Your Relationship Has to Offer."

Two friends suggested that we do a free evening presentation as a marketing strategy to generate attendees for our next seminar. So we booked a hotel room, advertised, and drew 28 people to attend for the evening.

We gave our presentation, but only one person registered for the weekend seminar.

> **Jim:** I was very disappointed. We gave an excellent presentation with so small a result.

We asked our friends, who happened to be marketers, what happened. Why didn't we get more registrations?

They said we didn't sell.

What?

They told us we didn't paint a picture of what someone would experience if they attended; we didn't tell them about others who had benefitted from having attended; we didn't excite them and persuade them to sign right up.

> **Judith:** I was devastated. It sounded like they were telling us to do all the things I hated about selling. Create phony emotions, get all fake excited, exaggerate. I cried all the way home.

Our friends were not particularly helpful. They talked in results. What they never told us was that we had to educate, inspire, and love what we had to offer. In other words, we had to prepare our audience members to buy.

We had no idea. We were therapists, after all. Had we understood this basic principle, we would have:

- Experienced a visceral connection to what our friends were telling us;

- Understood that, when done well, marketing is all about preparing your prospective customers so they can make the decision to buy;

- Made the benefits of buying clear to our audience members, so they would have a solid ground upon which to confidently take the action they wanted to take; and

- Assured them that what we offered would produce the results they were looking for.

But we didn't. We were a perfect example of not knowing what we were doing as marketers.

So we say it again—the essence of marketing is Preparing Your Customer to Buy. If you don't you are shortchanging your customers, yourself, and the success of your business.

So What About You?

You're reading this book because, more than likely, you are a soft sell marketer. You want to get your message into the world and make a living commensurate with your value, and the value of your products and services. We want that for you as well.

So, to say it again, as a marketer you are Preparing Your Customer to Buy, whether in the long term—with an introductory blog post or tweet—or in the immediate moment—on your sales page, over the phone, or in your office or store. Understanding what the job entails, what marketing is really all about, will save you no end of frustration to say nothing of unnecessary expense. When you open to this essential fact you open a larger possibility that you will succeed far beyond where your current desire will take you.

#2.   Who are soft sell marketers?

To understand whether or not you're likely to be a soft sell marketer—think of it this way. It's all about the difference between ROI and ROE.

ROI

If someone buys your product or service and they expect that the amount of money they pay you will return to them plus a profit, that's a Return on Investment or ROI transaction.

The intent on both sides—the seller and buyer—is an increase in money. So it's fundamentally a money-for-money exchange.

The sole purpose of this exchange is the accumulation and increase in the amount of money over and above that with which both buyer and seller entered into the transaction.

ROE

Now imagine that you are a parenting counselor and a young couple brings you their 5-year old. She's having difficulty adjusting to school. You give them guidance and it works. The child begins to enjoy school.

When they hand you their check, do they expect the amount of the check to return to them plus a profit? Of course not. That's not the nature of the exchange.

What you've done is facilitate a change in their life experience. The young couple wanted the quality of their life to be different and you helped them make that happen. That's why they're paying you.

For that kind of life-change transaction we use the term Return of Experience or ROE. Soft sell marketers, for the most part, specialize in ROE transactions.

ROE marketers include all health providers from MDs to energy healers, every kind of therapist, coach and counselor, life enhancement specialists like interior designers, wedding consultants, home school experts, recreation and travel professionals, musicians, artists, and a nearly endless list of specialists devoted to improving people's lives.

Soft Sell ROI

It's important to note that some ROE marketers also conduct soft sell ROI transactions.

They offer products and services that support ROE marketers including info-product creation, business development, blog and commercial website design, article writing for marketing purposes, softsell/softtopic copywriting, soft sell branding, teleseminar training, first step Internet marketing, and the like. Their intent is to help ROE marketers develop and grow their businesses.

These soft sell ROI marketers focus on the internal as well as the external elements of marketing, because they know marketing is not an exclusively external endeavor.

In our current role, we are soft sell ROI marketers.

We provide the emotional, psychological, and spiritual permission soft sell marketers need to grow themselves and their businesses far beyond what they imagine. So in our blog we use the slogan—"Marketing with Consciousness and Conscience"—aligning soft sell marketers' personal integrity with their best business practices. (http://www.bridgingheartandmarketing.com/blog)

#3. What is the primary benefit of soft sell marketing?

When traditional marketers think or talk about marketing they focus on the externals—price, packaging, discounts, refund policies, conversion rates, sales charting, bonuses, and, of course, the guarantee. Online, these marketers also concentrate on tracking, split-testing, email delivery rates, and, of course, list building.

Marketers, online and off, see the benefits of their marketing efforts in dollars-and-cents. That's how business has been defined. And every one of those external elements is vitally important.

However, there is an internal side to marketing that is much more rewarding than just the excitement of making more money or the vanity of dominating the competition. For the soft sell marketer and the soft sell marketplace the internals are of equal if not more importance.

Your Integrity

Integrity is the primary internal benefit you enjoy as a soft sell marketer—personal and professional integrity. You don't have to split off your desire to create and sustain a substantial income from your equal desire to treat your customers and potential customers with dignity, respect, and care.

Integrity is about being whole—living within a unity between what you believe and what you do, who you are and what you want, how you treat your customers and how you expect to be treated.

Doing business with integrity goes a long way to eliminate conflicting intentions. For example:

- You will create clear and coherent messages. Being out of integrity often leads to mixed and confusing messages because you are in conflict with yourself;

- Your prospective customer will not have to struggle to recognize and understand who you are and what you provide. Being out of integrity often makes it virtually impossible for your customers to easily identify with you; and

- Conflicting intentions create confusion and cause no end of frustration. They can lead to discouragement, disenchantment, and the downfall of your business.

Whereas clarity and sincerity are the hallmarks of marketing with integrity, leaving your customers with a sense of:

- security—you can be believed;

- promise—your product or service will deliver what you say it will;

- connection—you truly do know and understand them; and

- loyalty—you've proven to be trustworthy and they will return to buy again.

That's why soft sell marketers are just as influenced by the internal elements of marketing as they are by the externals. With harmony between both, you can confidently enjoy moving forward in the marketplace, providing the needed value you have to offer.

At an Arm's Length

The traditional protocol of emotionally keeping an arm's length between you, the seller, and your buyer—as a way of objectifying the sales process—reduces the experience of human connection in the exchange.

It's accepted as gospel that injecting anything personal, especially emotion, into the transaction will only muddy the outcome at best, or create a legal nightmare at worst. So selling and buying become an abstraction, with neither party responsible for the well-being of the other except in as much as that sentiment is required to consummate the sale.

But we've spoken to hundreds of care-givers, ROE life-enhancement artists, who market (or want to market) online, and they've told us that the typical, arm's length transaction doesn't work for them. It goes against their experience of and their need for the fundamental connectedness between people. Conducting business at an arm's length breaks the interpersonal wholeness at the center of their experience of being alive.

The connection, even on the Internet where the buyer and seller may never know each other, is based on a sense of person-to-person closeness and the intention of creating a long term relationship.

Accumulation Not Connection

Now, typical ROI hard sell marketing stands on its own fundamental integrity. It's an integrity based on accumulation not connection— except, as we said, inasmuch as some degree of connection is necessary to make the sale.

We know of a man whose companies make multi-millions every year. He's the envy of the Internet marketplace. His product? He dispenses advice to men on how to make their way with women by keeping the woman off-balance.

As former therapists, who for years worked to repair the damage between men and women due to the "counsel" they received on the "street," we see the consequences of this type of advice as deeply damaging to the relationship between the genders.

From all that we know of the man, there is no evidence that he suffers any internal conflict between what he does and the money it makes for him. Quite the contrary. He is an accumulation artist and a very successful one. Money is the signal measure of his authority and success. He doesn't suffer conflicting intentions because he operates his business from only one dimension of consequence—profit. So, within that one dimension, he is in integrity.

But the dissociation, the fracture between money earned and the emotional impact delivered, is what soft sell marketers cannot live with. It tears at the alignment between personal and professional integrity. It creates a psychic split that is ultimately self-destructive.

A Balance Between Commerce and Conscience

When someone buys a product or makes use of a service there are always residual emotional, psychological, and spiritual effects that endure long-term, well after the transaction is complete.

For example, as we write this passage we are at the automobile dealership waiting for our 7500-mile servicing to be completed. This transaction doesn't end when we drive off the lot. It carries forward as we drive with a sense of protection—trusting that we received expert care—and a sense of safety—that the car is in reliable mechanical condition.

As a result we drive with a sense of ease, allowing us, as we're driving, to focus on our conversation, the radio or CD entertainment, or the scenery if we're in the country, rather than needing to think about the car. Of course our sense of security and safety is not in the forefront of our consciousness. We take it for granted. But it's there nonetheless.

And it's these long-term internal effects that bring us back to the same dealership. They form the basis of our relationship and why we drive across town when, in fact, we could have the work done at a similar dealership nearby.

In truth, we are never out of connection with our dealership, nor they with us—even though the connection is predominantly unconscious. It's subtle, psychological, perhaps even spiritual, depending on the depth of connection. And when we think about it, it adds a quality of conscience to both sides of the relationship.

The soft sell marketers we've spoken with are conscious of, sensitive to, and take very seriously the long-term effects of their products and services on the emotional and spiritual well-being of their customers. For them, success is the balance between commerce and conscience.

You see, in fact, the connectedness is always present and that means there is no such thing as an arm's length transaction.

The Soft Sell Marketplace

The soft sell marketplace is huge. So there's no need to copy the hard sell approach. It won't work for you. We know. It never worked for us.

Instead, for your own well-being, stay true to who you are. Then, as you practice soft sell marketing, you will live within the integrity of unifying what you believe with what you do in the world, joining together money earned and the value you provide to your clients and customers.

Only by staying true to your deepest personal values will you care best for your customers and generate the income you deserve for the value you bring to those who need what you provide. And you'll do so with a sound emotional and spiritual conscience.

#4. How has your business changed since you started soft sell marketing?

Prior to taking over the writing of our own sales copy for our dating program, which we mentioned earlier, we tried promoting our relationship programs following the harder sell methodologies. False scarcity. Pushy urgency. Hit the pain hard, hard, hard.

But in promoting our first major product "Smart Dating for Success Every Time— Guaranteed!" we moved in the direction of soft sell marketing. (http://www.judithandjim.com/smartdating)

Think about it. If you are single, seriously desiring a long term committed relationship, and already feeling frustrated, you certainly don't want someone sending you sales copy that will make you feel worse. It's already a painful, even maddening place to find yourself in.

So we knew we needed a better way to speak with our readers about their dating challenges and the life-changing benefits of our program. And that set us on the path to developing the soft sell marketing approach.

Never Imagined We'd Be Where We Are

As we've said, from speaking with our copywriting students—all care-givers, change agents of one kind or another—and the people we met at Internet conferences who also didn't fit in, we knew there had to be some way we could contribute to and support the personal and professional growth of soft sell marketers for whom the hard sell approach simply doesn't fit.

So we took a leap of faith!

In mid-2007 we decided to put on an Internet conference dedicated to the needs of the soft sell community. Several people told us we were crazy, that we'd lose tons of money because the hotel was expensive, the videographer was expensive, and our event coordinator was expensive—and those were all hard costs.

But we knew we had to do it.

When we did our promotional tele-calls, Judith invariably became tearful speaking about how much it meant to provide this type of support for our fellow soft sell community members.

Jim felt a passion rarely experienced except through philosophy and poetry.

It touched us deeply. Soul-deeply. We never imagined we'd be doing this. But we knew we'd been drawn into something larger than who we'd been, and we had to follow wherever it would (and continues to) lead us.

We called the conference "Bridging Heart and Marketing," and it was a huge success—on every level. Those who attended continue to rave about it. The speakers were impressed. And we made a profit. A good profit.

We gave "Bridging Heart and Marketing II" later in 2008 and it was also a seriously huge success.

The Soft Sell Marketers Association

Our vision for what we're doing has expanded far beyond the gathering-together of colleagues and the training that occurs at our conferences. We now see the need to harness the power of the soft sell marketing community to influence world commerce.

After all, commerce is one of the most basic communication tools we have. As we conduct commerce, so goes the world. So in October 2008 we opened the doors to the Soft Sell Marketers Association (SSMA).

Beginning immediately as an international organization with members in Germany, Mexico, Canada, and Australia, the SSMA is a training ground, support center, and gathering place for connections between and among soft sell marketers.

And as it grows, so grows the world of heart-based, soul-supported commerce.

Finally . . . The Money

Everyone always wants to know if there's money to be made in soft sell marketing. The answer, sweet and simple: Yes there is!

To give you a glimpse of what is possible, we started by taking Alex Mandossian's first Teleseminar Secrets course which ended in February 2005. Before that we had *no* sales or marketing training or background and *no* tech-ability.

From that point on these are our gross income figures:

- Pre soft sell marketing: in 2005 we made $32,000.

- Teaching "Soft Topic Copywriting Secrets" and other soft sell programs—in 2006 we made $87,000 and in 2007 – $103,000.

- Opening the doors to "Bridging Heart and Marketing," in 2008 we made over $250,000.

Is there money to be made and still remain within your own personal and professional soft sell integrity? The numbers speak for themselves. And this is just the beginning for all of us.

#5.   How did you come across the name soft sell marketing?

In our Introduction "From Therapists to Marketers" we mentioned that it was Alex Mandossian who referred to our program "Smart Dating for Success Every Time – Guaranteed!" as a soft topic. And we also mentioned that he gave us the title "Soft Topic Copywriting Secrets" for our copywriting course, which we still use for our home study course.

However, as we expanded our understanding of the market we wanted to serve, creating our initial "Bridging Heart and Marketing" Internet marketing conference February 2008, we realized that we weren't so much addressing the issue of "soft topics" as we were addressing a particular style of selling—no matter what the topic of someone's product or service might be.

It was the abuses and extremes of hard sell marketing that motivated us to create another orientation toward marketing and sales. Since "hard sell" is a description that's commonly used, it became obvious that what we were creating was the other side of the coin—soft sell.

So then we knew we needed to change the way we were labeling and talking about what we were doing—from soft topic to soft sell.

And that's how "Soft Sell Marketing" came to be.

Simple as that.

#6. How does soft sell marketing differ from hard sell?

There are many differences between soft and hard sell, and we will detail them as we answer the rest of the questions in this book. But here we want to describe a core difference from which all the other differences follow.

It's the difference between emotional connection and mental technique.

An Emotional Decision

A bottom line truth in marketing and sales is that people buy emotionally and justify logically. In other words, buying is fundamentally an emotional decision not a mental act.

To illustrate the power of this difference we turn to the world of acting where there are two major schools of thought about how an actor can best move an audience with his/her performance.

Method Acting teaches actors to draw their performances out of their own real life experiences. This leads the actor to actually feel the emotions the character feels in the situations of the play or film.

If the actor is literally experiencing the feelings that are appropriate to what the character goes through the chance that an audience will believe the performance and be moved emotionally will be high—because the performance will be authentic and, therefore, believable.

Technique Acting relies on the application of a set of techniques—vocal modulation, gesture, line readings, etc.—that give the appearance of what the character is going through without the actor actually experiencing it.

The risk with this approach is that it lowers the chance that the audience will be moved because the performance won't be as believable. The audience is watching a mental performance rather than something emotionally real so the likelihood of their becoming emotionally involved drops precipitously.

Now, how can these two approaches be used in looking at a sales document?

Believability

The goal of any of your sales documents is to emotionally convince your readers that the product you're offering will do what your writing claims it will do and that they will receive all the benefits you promise. You want the sales letter to be so believable that it moves your readers to take the action they want to take and you want them to take so that they buy your product.

Given that, which approach do you think has the best chance for success:

> A sales letter that comes directly out of your sincere and authentic experience, filled with the feelings you actually feel about the product or service?

> Or a letter that's been written using techniques that are supposed to give the appearance of your authenticity and genuine expression?

The Internet is jam-packed with pages and pages of "techniqued" documents that, although they work for a certain segment of the marketplace, they are a death knell for the soft sell consumer. They feel like hype because they are predominantly mental, void of sincere connection.

Only Mentally Involved

There's an emotional distance, even an emotional absence inherent in a technique-driven sales letter. That's because the writer is only mentally involved. It's only an appearance. To get beyond that distance the writer has to overstate, embroider, bend the truth, or create gimmicks to compensate for the lack of genuine feeling.

In order to stimulate action, the writer has to rely on and impose an inauthentic urgency— "Orders are coming in like crazy. Don't miss out!"

Or an inauthentic scarcity—"Only 23 copies of this eBook are available. SO ACT NOW!"

For the soft sell customer, reading this kind of copy leaves a bad taste because it's mostly emotional manipulation.

Let Your Feelings Come Through

When you let your real feelings come through your sales promotions—whether written or spoken—you have a high probability of creating a real connection with your prospective customers because you are believable. Your genuine emotional experience of loving your customer is the basis of your authenticity and your offer. And your open, direct, and honest expression is the basis of the connection both you and your reader are looking for. You won't need to manipulate because you speak from your heartfelt authority.

#7. Is technique necessary in writing soft sell sales copy?

Yes, technique is absolutely necessary in order to write effective sales copy.

And because, in our answer to Question #6, we warned against a "techniqued" approach to writing sales copy, we feel it's necessary to focus on the technical elements of copywriting so we don't give the impression that you should disregard technique.

Sales letters, and, for that matter, any written sales documents, have but one objective—to move readers to take an action—that is, to purchase your offer. So your letter cannot be an arbitrary flow of words or a stream of consciousness. It must be structured to accomplish that end. That's where technique comes in.

At the Movies

When you go to the movies you expect to become involved in a story. To capture and keep your attention screen writers structure their scripts with a beginning, middle, and end—helping you follow the flow of the plot and the action. So a screenplay is usually divided into three acts.

Within those acts the writer employs various techniques to keep you watching: reversals, surprises, revelations, romance, chase scenes, a powerful climax to name just a few. If the writer doesn't use some or all of those techniques the story won't keep your attention and cannot move you emotionally.

However, what if you go to see a slasher movie or a romantic comedy, a family drama or a war film? Each one is based on the same chronology—

beginning, middle, and end—and laced with techniques to hold your attention and sway your emotions.

Yet it's obvious that each of those movie genres is very, very different. What makes the difference? Obviously, it's the central plot or story. But it's also the tone or voice of the screenplay. It's the outer manifestation of the story teller's intention to create a very specific experience for the audience, providing an equally specific emotional response at the end.

Invitation vs Command

With soft sell marketing your intention is to create and maintain an authentic, heartfelt emotional connection with your customers while leading them through your sales presentation—all the while preparing your customers to buy what you offer.

An Internet or direct soft sell sales letter is more like an invitation. A hard sell sales letter is more like an implicit—and sometimes explicit—command.

For example, a very well known, and very successful hard sell copywriter describes his potential reader as "A five-hundred pound slob sitting on a couch eating popcorn and watching television. It's the writer's job to get that slob off the couch, pull out his credit card, and buy the product."

If that's in fact the case, just imagine the kind of language the writer must use and the brow-beating he must deliver to get the action he wants from the guy on the couch. It only makes sense that his copy has to be aggressive, abusive, even assaultive.

Instead, soft sell marketers begin with the view that their prospective customer is first and foremost a person to be respected. There's no need for hammering. In fact, hammering goes against the marketer's personal and professional integrity.

A hard sell approach, with language like "killer copy," "crush your competition," and "you're a moron if you don't buy this right now" goes against the soft sell marketer's sense of personal integrity. It also insults the customer as well as the product being offered.

Solid Writing Technique

So in order to achieve the appropriate, caring, and sincere emotional tone in your sales copy as well as promote and complete the desired sale, a combination of heartfelt openness and solid writing technique is necessary to:

- Create the connection necessary for the reader to establish an emotional identification with you as well as the trust needed to maintain a long term relationship, and

- Lead the reader through your sales presentation in a logical, cohesive manner so that he or she clearly and completely understands the value your offer provides and what they have to do next—which is to purchase your product or service.

Effective and persuasive soft sell copywriting is a blend of structured technique and sincere, personal emotional connection. Both are essential to meeting your readers where they are at the moment they bring their hopes to your offer. The magic of that moment depends on your use of appropriate technique.

There's a huge difference between writing with technique and a "techniqued" writer. As a soft sell marketer the latter won't work over the long term. Only by sincerely expressing the truth of who you are from a base of feeling for and genuine connection with your customers and clients will you be able to turn your writing into persuasive and convincing sales documents.

So, is technique necessary? Yes, absolutely.

For more information about our Soft Topic Copywriting Secrets Home Study Course, go to:

(http://www.softtopiccopywritingsecrets.com)

#8. How can you say that selling is spiritual service?

Earlier we shared with you how Jim discovered the idea that selling is spiritual service. But that concept may seem foreign to you, even impossible. So what we've said bears repeating. And now we'll go more deeply into what we mean by Selling Is Spiritual Service.

This perspective on selling is based on the profound reality that we are all connected. We are all one interconnected web of consciousness. We all create together the experience of being alive, so we all need each other. That's a simple and profound fact of life.

As John Donne wrote in the seventeenth century, "No man is an island."

When someone has a problem they can't solve by themselves—and you have a solution in the form of a product or service—you have an ethical, even moral obligation to make your solution available to as many people as you can.

If you don't, you shortchange your own creative spirit as well as your business. You shortchange all the people who need what you provide. And you shortchange Spirit or God, or whatever it is you deem to be The Source of All.

This point of view is fundamental to your larger success as a soft sell marketer, and *The Heart of Marketing* is devoted to supporting you and the growth and expansion of your heart-based marketing.

So let's look at this more closely.

What Is Selling?

Selling is the process of converting someone from being a looker, a seeker, a searcher, a prospector into becoming a Customer.

It's the art and skill of helping your reader make the decision they know they need and want to make in order to solve the problem they're wrestling with. The selling process guides them to that decision for the benefit of both of you.

As a soft sell marketer, when you add the commitment to sell with respect and care, your priority becomes the well-being of the relationship between you and your buyer, which also includes the sale.

What Is Spiritual?

At the core, practical spirituality takes us to the fundamental connectedness that permeates and creates this world and the need we all have of one another. When you take in the emotional truth of our interdependence—and let it guide your business dealings—you begin to market and sell with consciousness and conscience.

> Consciousness—with awareness of the co-creative life
> that joins us all together, the customer becomes not
> just someone who will buy, but a necessary partner in
> determining the best outcome for both you and your buyer.

> Conscience—reflects the care and respect for ourselves
> and our customers as feeling-filled human beings, not just
> walking wallets.

Doing business with consciousness and conscience you advance the experience of being alive by recognizing and supporting the well-being of the whole—the whole of life on this planet through the whole transaction—that is, your awareness of both the seller and the buyer.

When you participate in a spiritually motivated sale you recognize the gifts you, the seller, bring to the marketplace as well as the need brought by your buyer. There is a unity of purpose and respect that is expressed through and manifested in a value-for-value exchange.

What Is Service?

Service is the assistance you offer as you put yourself forward to support and advance your prospective customer's buying experience. When in service, you contribute to the well-being of your prospective customer even if they never become a buyer.

However, when you come from service, you must avoid martyring yourself. To fully participate in the buyer/seller partnership you must make sure to serve your own self-expression, your own personal value, and your own economic well-being. Otherwise you negate the partnership and are thrust back into the every-man-for-himself mindset. It's essential that you respect and support *both* you *and* your customer.

When you take to heart that Selling Is Spiritual Service you are on your way to release from fear, shyness, embarrassment, guilt and any other internal millstone holding you back from marketing with passionate commitment. You are emboldened to use your marketing to educate your readers about what you know, what you've created for them, and you invite and encourage them to make the decision they already know they want to make.

You share your story, you outline the many benefits they can enjoy, and you provide testimonials from satisfied customers so that your readers know, truly know they are in the right place. Then when they buy, when they put money in your bank, their payment is a form of appreciation and gratitude.

That's the power of Selling As Spiritual Service.

#9. I've heard you use the term "soul-based business." What is a soul-based business?

At our Bridging Heart and Marketing II conference we addressed the idea of a soul-based business as the basis for the work we now do. We're aware that "soul-based business" isn't yet a common term. Nevertheless, running your business from a soul perspective is fundamental to achieving the level of success and satisfaction that you, as a soft sell marketer, are after.

So, Just What Is A "Soul-Based Business"?

We're not interested in a philosophical or theological definition. Instead we have a 7-point, practical description that you can apply to your own business.

1) When your soul is touched, you've reached the stillpoint at the center of your deepest personal truth. Although this sounds non-businessy, it's actually the result of your determined effort to answer the question "What specifically do I have to offer?" This question can be re-framed to ask, "Why should someone buy from me instead of anyone else?" Your persistence to touch the truth leads to the discovery and articulation of who you are in your business and the uniqueness of what you bring to the market.

2) At your stillpoint you become aware of how your truth fits into the collective consciousness, the collective unconscious, and the wisdom of the cosmic order. Why? Because you

are a member of the connectedness. With commitment and persistence, you will know your unique place in the connectedness. And you will know your answer to "What is my position in the market I serve?"

3) From within your awareness a vision arises, a clear picture of what your business is, what it offers, who it helps, and the connection between you and your specific audience. It's your answer to the question "How exactly does what I do recognize and resolve the needs of those in my specific audience?"

4) Because of your deeper awareness and understanding, your business ceases being merely head-based—that is a collection of concepts and techniques that keep you at a distance from yourself and those you want as customers. It's a genuinely soul-based vision arising from who you are at the depth of your connectedness, your interdependence with all of life. It answers the question: "What does this business mean to me and what does it do for my life and the lives of my customers?"

5) Your vision then moves into your heart—the feeling field. It is through your heart-feeling that you can most deeply and most meaningfully connect with those around you as you transact your business and your daily life, discovering the answer to: "How do I extend out beyond myself and place my offer into the marketplace and attract those who are looking for me?"

6) Next, your vision moves into consciousness, where you articulate the specifics of who you are and what you offer so that your message can be clearly conveyed to those who are looking for you. "How do I verbalize, clearly and distinctly, what I offer and its numerous benefits so I am identifiable by those who I am committed to serving?"

7) And finally your vision becomes physical through the products and/or services you create, expressing the

uniqueness that you are. Unique, not because you've measured yourself against everyone else in your market niche and created something you believe is different—you are unique from within, from that base of who you are. Your particular products and services are the personal expression of what began in the stillness of your soul.

Your Life's Mission

When you operate a soul-based business, your work becomes your life mission instead of a day job that you hope will someday give you the freedom to finally live your mission. Your business has been spiritualized and you are connected, multi-dimensionally, to your inner world, to the world around you, and to whatever you hold as The Highest Value In Creation.

When you are in touch with your soul you are guided by something much larger than: • fear, • habit, • need, • your personal history, • what everybody else expects of you, • or even what you think you *should* be doing.

When you are living a soul-based business, your soul will prompt you to discover more and more of who you really are and specifically how you can serve as many people as possible.

Scare Yourself To Life

Rather than scare you to death, your soul will Scare You To Life. Your soul will push you beyond previous limitations of imagination and skill, connections and financing to leap into a greater future than you've been able to see on your own. And your soul will give you the courage and clarity to follow the vision and requirements of your soul-calling.

That's the beauty of your soul-based business. It provides the vehicle for your personal growth all the while guiding you to grow your business beyond what you've previously imagined. Because a soul-based business goes beyond just doing business for the sake of making a living. It moves you to make a larger and deeper impact on the world.

What Do You Need to Do Now?

It's now time for a personal inventory as the first step toward arriving at your stillpoint. So, given your expertise and your current business status:

- What do you need to do so that you can follow the calling of your soul?

- How do you need to take the risks you've been avoiding in order to have the business of your dreams?

- How can your soul help you step out so you can impact the world around you in just the right way?

If you are to achieve the largest success and impact you desire, take these questions seriously. Your answers provide the internal base for your marketing success and satisfaction.

If you want to explore this issue further, listen to our audio program "How Do You Know Your Soul Calling?"

(http://www.judithandjim.com/soulcalling)

#10. Why Do You Say That A Soul-Based Business Is A Spiritual Teacher?

When you open yourself to connecting with your soul as the foundation for creating your business, you open yourself to the larger creative forces that await to help you move beyond what has been. You step into what you have not as yet imagined and become an explorer of your own particular genius and your service to the rest of humanity.

You live out your discoveries through your work and, in that light, your work becomes more than just the accumulation of money. It becomes a spiritual teacher.

In other words—as you build your business, you grow your Self.

For example, you are made more and more whole through what your soul requires of you as you pursue the growth of your business. This is not accomplished merely through external techniques—how to improve your advertising and lead generation, how to better drive traffic, write more effective subject lines, or install and apply the latest video software.

All of that is important. Critically so. But if your business is only idea-based—that is, strictly cognitive and concept-based—new techniques may generate some results, but you're left chasing the latest glittering technical bauble, the latest "sure-to-make-you-rich" scheme. In other words, you're left chasing what other people are doing.

A Change In Your DNA

As a soul-based entrepreneur and marketer, the source of your business success emerges from within, from your ongoing and careful listening to what is right for you and right for your customers.

The result of your careful listening is that your soul shows you how to fill in the holes in your psyche, in your heart, in your presence on this planet. Holes of ignorance, prejudice, or unconscious self-limitations that keep you off-balance, never quite comfortable in your own skin, begin to fill in and create a new internal platform for your future success.

Filling in the holes is not merely a matter of mental shifting. It's not a matter of scrambling to stay ahead of a changing business world. When you are soul-based, you possess a solid yet flexible internal center. You possess an emotional/spiritual/commercial gyroscope so that you can turn freely in any or all directions, yet keep oriented in the way that is best for you and your customers.

When you make a change according to your soul's lead you don't merely change direction, you expand into a different way of being in the world. Your brain function literally grows as your synapses evolve and you change your emotional and spiritual DNA.

Judith the Techno-Phobe

As we've said, we entered the world of Internet marketing after Judith heard Alex Mandossian on a promotional tele-conference. The idea of marketing appealed to her, but she had no idea—NO IDEA—what she was getting into from the computer technology side.

She was prompted by a deeper impulse than just the Internet as a way of making money. Her soul called to her, although she didn't know it at the time.

Did she have to learn to use the computer waaaaay beyond just email and word processing? Certainly. She had to make friends with it. And that pushed her right up against an internal roadblock she'd struggled with her whole life.

A Deep Resistance

As a child who was severely criticized when she didn't get something right, right away, she developed a deep resistance to learning. If it didn't come easily, she didn't bother. And learning the computer did not come easily. Not at all.

> **Judith:** Again and again I raged, wept, and fell into deep hopelessness, because I could find in no part of me a connection with the logic of the computer. It was alien to me. Yet I had to learn.

And she learned—under an intense emotional demand to confront and release her knee-jerk, uncompromising stance against needing to learn—which, ultimately had less to do with computer logic and everything to do with a deeply habituated defense against the pain she'd buried as a child.

For Judith this was no mere mental shift but a shift into a new way of being in the world—a restructuring of her emotional and spiritual DNA. Her soul-driven choice to market on the Internet led her into the necessity of having to use the complexities of the computer to do so. And that decision was ultimately far more about her need to substantially change her prejudice against learning so she could move forward.

> **Judith:** Internet marketing has been the best therapist I've ever had.

In truth it was her own determination, her own soul calling that became her best therapist, but the medium was the alien world of computer technology.

> **Judith:** I felt pushed, prodded, sometimes bullied into having not only to learn, but learn a way of thinking that was completely foreign to me. I had to grow beyond my fears, my past, my distorted imaginings in order to make Internet marketing succeed.

That's just one example of how our soul-based business has been a spiritual teacher.

Obstacles Overcome

Today, we not only market and sell on the Internet:

- We successfully produce Bridging Heart and Marketing, the only Internet marketing conference for soft sell Internet marketers.
  (http://www.bridgingheartandmarketing.com);

- We've created the Soft Sell Marketers Association where success and spirituality join together for the benefit of all.
  (http://www.softsellmarketersassociation.org);

- We offer our Soft Topic Copywriting Secrets home study course, the only copywriting course for the soft sell market.
  (http://www.softtopiccopywritingsecrets.com);

- We market our program Overcoming the Fear of Being Fabulous to help and support those who struggle with internal resistance to moving ahead in their business and in their lives.
  (http://www.overcomingthefearofbeingfabulous.com); and

- We provide our 3-day intensive Magnify Your Excellence to support your specific genius while we dig deep into what needs to be released. The possibility of greater personal and professional success is expanded and transformed into a reality you can see and feel (http://www.magnifyyourexcellence.com).

Plus other programs too numerous to list here.

And What About You?

As you are challenged to move into areas that are "not my thing," "too far afield for someone like me," or "never going to be enjoyable," how are you invited to grow beyond your current understanding and experience of who you are? Because, as you push into the challenge, you will:

- Notice how—little by little—those holes in your character become apparent, compelling you to face into them;
- Notice how with care-filled awareness, opening to what has been long buried, you begin to uncover, understand, rearrange, and change what has been holding you back, taking what has been an impediment and turning it into a support;
- Notice how your business takes on new dimensions of success that were not available to you before you accepted the spiritual challenge of filling in your Holes and becoming more Whole.

We recommend that you keep a journal of business successes that emerge from and are a reflection of your personal growth, and vice versa.

Doing so you will: • make the fleeting thoughts, feelings, intuitions, and inspirations real and concrete by putting them on paper; and • document the various ways a soul-based business can be a spiritual teacher opening you to being more and more of who you are, who you really, really are.

#11. What are the bottom line principles of soft sell marketing?

While some people express concern that soft sell marketing might be seen by their customers as "airy-fairy" or too "touchy-feely," or as Mark Joyner called it "hoofy poofy," as a soft sell marketer you need not worry when you rely on the following spiritually grounded principles.

1) Selling Is Spiritual Service

Understanding that selling is spiritual service re-frames, to the core, what selling is all about.

Because when you sell from the perspective of spiritual service, you cannot help but keep your prospective customers' best interests at heart as well as your own. Understanding and having a feeling for the interdependence we all live within, you avoid any risk of becoming greed-driven, focused solely on your competitive interests, disregarding the long-term residual impact of your actions on the well-being of others.

When you take care that you are selling from a base of spiritual service—acknowledging the partnership quality of any sale—then selling becomes a process of care and connection in which mutuality and reciprocity are the moral codes you follow in your business dealings.

But we want to be very clear. We're not talking about "reciprocity" as a sales trigger to be exploited. As a soft sell marketer, you don't give to your prospective customers as a "reciprocity technique" to trigger the feeling that they have to give back. Instead, genuine reciprocity is a fundamental concept for healthy commercial relationships and good business.

2) How You Perceive Your Potential Customer

Your customer is not a concept. He or she is not a conversion percentage, not a lead, not part of your herd, not an abstract psyche you want to manipulate, not a target with a sweet spot to be tapped.

Your customer is a human being whose needs, wants, fears and joys are as important to him/her as yours are to you. In creating your products and/or services, your marketing campaigns, your sales letters, emails, and whatever else you need to market and sell what you offer, it's essential that you include, along with all of the external techniques of marketing, a visceral sense of respect and care for the very real humanness of the people you are marketing to. Otherwise marketing becomes an abstraction, devoid of real people, and then it's only about the numbers. That opens the door for abuse.

3) Your Emotional Connection with Your Customer Is the Basis of Your Business

Because your emotional connection with your customer is the basis of your soft sell business success, you don't exploit human emotion with techniques that excite, inflame, or provoke your potential customer into buying what you offer. Human emotions are not merely trigger points you agitate just to make a sale. As a soft sell marketer you know that human emotions are sensitive and vulnerable to being hyped so you must respect them throughout the sales process. If you resort to hype, you expose your disrespect, and that borders on contempt, abusing the trust and care that's at the center of every well made sale.

To create and keep your long-term customer connections, emotional respect is key. Because the safety and satisfaction your customer either feels or senses is grounded in their conscious or unconscious response to how you treat them—depending on whether they experience a sense of respectful and caring emotional intimacy—or a felt distance, even danger.

Emotional safety, deeply a part of every spiritually-based sale, allows you to engage openly with your customer so that both of you are well treated and well cared for.

4) You Can Match Your Message to the Heart of Your Market

When you match your message to the heart of your market, you connect with the emotional center of your customer's needs and wants. If you use just cognitive, conceptual arguments to boost the value of what you offer, you're not standing on solid ground.

For example, many marketers rely on price discounts as a customer hook. But the truth is, anyone can give a discount. Anyone can extend the time period of their guarantee. Anyone can promise benefits by the list full. But when there's no heart-to-heart connection, your customer remains a mere fish on a hook.

Soft sell success is based on the intensity and richness of feeling—your internal connection with your self and your buyer—which you then couple with good pricing, solid guarantees, believable benefits, and the rest of the external elements that make up your personal selling proposition.

Your internal availability is the key that creates a spiritual connection at the heart of every mutually enjoyable and beneficial sale.

5) A Sale Is a Sacred Moment

That a sale can be a sacred moment may sound as if we've gone too far. But think about it.

When someone comes to you because they need your solution and they've chosen your offer from a field of products and services that are similar to what you provide, their purchase is not arbitrary. They've decided that yours is the solution that best fits their needs.

So, when they've purchased and then applied your solution—and it works—they're not able to be separate from you. They don't just make use of your product and then they're gone. Instead, they've taken you—through your solution—into their own very real life. Now they are carrying you with them well beyond the moment of purchase. You have become part of their life. The sale has now been transformed from merely a commercial exchange to one that is sacred. The more serious the problem the deeper your presence is within them and the more sacred the relationship between you.

The sacred is housed within the connectedness that is present in advance of a sale and is made vivid when your customers use your solution to change their lives. You can't help but be with them because they have taken you in and have constellated some part of themselves around you.

Also, because they've placed their trust in you through your solution, no matter how much you, as a marketer, would like to protect yourself through the concept of buyer beware, you have an implicit moral responsibility, to say nothing of the sound business practice, to not violate that trust.

Yes, your customer is also responsible, but this book is about you, the marketer. And when you do what you can to protect that trust through the authenticity and transperancy of your dealings, you are behaving within the sacred, because "sacred" means protected from violation.

Now, when your customer pays you, their money is not just currency. It's an act of appreciation, a statement of gratitude. When they send you a testimonial, that's another form of gratitude—not just "thanks," but gratitude for what you've done for them.

The nature of the transaction has a spiritual life all its own so that you can never, in good conscience, emotionally abuse your potential customer with disrespectful and demeaning marketing/sales techniques.

Instead, you are caring and respectful in what you say about your offer, how you say it, the transparency with which you allow yourself to be seen, and the authenticity that grounds the trust between you and your buyer—because a sale is a sacred moment.

#12. People say to succeed you have to get your ego out of the way. What does that mean?

This is a loaded question that can either lead down a black hole or toward the release of freedom that will support your business as well as your whole life. But first . . .

What Is Ego?

Ego is a term that's tossed around by a lot of people who have little notion of what it means and by professionals who proffer elaborate technical descriptions that end up not being very helpful. So our definition is intended to be practical and applicable to you—the soft sell marketer.

From infancy on we all make decisions and judgments about who we are and what life means to us. For example, here's a bottom-line question: "Is life friendly?" Your judgment in answer to this question has enormous implications for how your ego is formed and how you conduct your entire life.

If you decide that life is friendly you can be open, inquisitive, embracing of all the many opportunities to grow and develop. You can easily ask for help and receive it with grace. You can open to love and be loved as an everyday aspect of being alive. And you're likely to view success as eminently achievable, if not your birthright.

If you decide that life is not friendly, you are more than likely to shut down, become cynical and depressed. While you're apt to feel envious of others' success and happiness, the thought of growing out beyond where you are right now may seem far too dangerous. And your ego makes you hold back.

So your answer forms the basis of who you are and how you experience being alive.

Just Imagine

Imagine you've been forced to wear a pair of glasses with a bizarre prescription. They are reddish in color, one lens is thick and the other is just glass, the frames are heavy and black and wrap around your face so that you have little peripheral vision. What would the world look like?

Now imagine that you've had those glasses on your whole life but didn't know it. Your view of the world would seem normal to you, and you'd have no reason to question it.

That's what ego is like. It's the psychological lens you live with that's been formed by ideas, beliefs, attitudes, fears, hopes, decisions and judgments that are mostly unconscious. Your "ego lens" dictates what you will see and what you won't, what you can see and what you can't.

And the worst of it is, unless you become aware of how the limitations of your ego keep you confined and you do something about it, you'll remain mired within a point of view that hardens as you grow older, and not only gives you no reason to challenge it, but every reason to defend it mightily, even to death if necessary.

Ego and Soft Sell Marketing

Marketing is an ongoing, improvisational practice. It changes with the mood and needs of the times. As a marketer you need to be in tune with and ready to adjust to current conditions, whatever they may be. So you can't cling to what worked yesterday if it's not working today. That'll put you out of business. You have to adapt and evolve.

But when it comes to the ego, much of what has constellated to shape who you are and what you do is unconscious—noticeable only through repetitive behaviors, thoughts, and feelings.

It's the repetition that imprisons you in a process that won't allow you to open up and change. But it's also the repetition that gives you clues to what's keeping you stuck.

So does it profit you to get your ego out of the way? Definitely. Because, as you do, you will gain access to deeper creativity and inspiration, and allow yourself to better connect with your customers and prospective customers.

As we said in Question #9, you'll gain access to the collective consciousness and the wisdom of the cosmic order:

- Reviving your intuition;

- Expanding your imagination;

- Strengthening your sense of connection with your self and your customers;

- Allowing you to drop the burden of arm's length hard sell methods.

The more you step out of your ego and into the open-minded connection with those you serve, the more you will experience the truth that Selling Is Spiritual Service—for your customers as well as for your Self.

#13. I believe I have a great service to offer people but I have a very difficult time not wanting to ask "Are you nuts?" when they say they don't want to even look at the benefits.

Here's a simple answer to your question. Remember a time when you said "No" without even looking at the benefits. What were you feeling? What were you thinking? Would you have wanted to hear—"Are you nuts?" Unlikely. Right?

So the real question is—why didn't your visitors even want to look at the benefits of your offer?

Open the Relationship

We suspect that what you were doing was working to close the sale instead of opening the relationship and your visitors sensed that. To say it another way, your objective was misplaced and your potential customers could feel it.

Think about it. How do you perceive your prospective customers since you admit you have the impulse to blame them? That's not to say that your impulse is always wrong. But a better question to ask is—"What am I doing that results in their disinterest?"

We're not asking from some pedestal on-high. We've had your same impulse. But then we had to ask what benefit was there for our potential customers when we were trying to close the sale, treating them strictly as our source of income, rather than opening the relationship and treating them respectfully as people? Why should they have bothered to look?

So we changed our approach because the true success of any sale is in the ongoing, repeat business that follows. And that's all about the relationship, the authentic connection that's felt on both sides.

This is why we say—rather than "closing the sale" consider "opening the relationship." Because this shift in your consciousness will change everything.

Lack of Authority

We also suggest that you take a look at the lack of authority in your presentation. Because it appears that whatever you're doing isn't specific enough, not expert enough, not clear enough to bring forth in your prospective customers a vision of accomplishment, a feeling of excitement, and a sense of hope that you have what they need.

Let's look at these one at a time.

Authority and Specificity Are Synonymous

You've probably heard the maxim—God is in the details. In other words, the Supreme Creative Authority is recognized and known through the smallest and finest of details.

Why? Because it's the details that give a person, an object, or a presentation its recognizable character—its uniqueness. If you haven't defined and spelled out the details of what you offer, your product remains fuzzy and indistinct, not easy to grasp, not easy to imagine the benefits that you're making available.

We trust you know your benefits. But you're not getting them across well enough to those who are looking for you.

Expertise

When your prospective customers can't easily and immediately grasp what you're offering then your expertise suffers. You may be expert with respect to your product, but you're not expert in generating trust in and desire for what you provide.

Then any claim you make suffers—both with regard to your product, but more important, with regard to how you present yourself in the moment. That's where trust is established. Right here. Right now. Whether your audience is reading sales copy or listening to you in person, you must clearly put forth your expertise, making yourself readily and reliably available in the moment.

Clarity and Communication

When, from the depth of your expertise, you communicate your passionate soul-based commitment to what you do, that's when your prospective customer is most likely to be moved by your message. That's when your clarity is at its highest. There's no emotional, intellectual, or spiritual distance between you and your message, between your message and your specific audience.

The other person connects with you, and has no reason to *not* want to look at your benefits. Then it's not possible for you to have an impulse to blame them because they get you. In fact, they can't help but get you, because they know you get them, really, really get them and what they need or want. And if they don't, they're not your customers.

Your authority flows from your being specific about what you offer. That specificity reveals your deepest expertise and experience. When you communicate that with maximum clarity your prospective customer feels connected with you at a soul level and it's appealing and safe to follow you.

No Hype

Recently we spoke on the phone with a woman and her husband. She had been referred to us as possible mentors because our reputation for success and straightforwardness preceded us.

We had to disabuse her of several fantasies she'd concocted having heard the "You Can Do It Too!" get rich quick pitches on the Internet.

She was just barely getting started and asked if it was possible that in several months she could be making $5000 per month online.

Judith: I said that anything was possible but not likely.

Jim: I said, "I don't mean to take the excitement out of your ambition but the probability of $5000 in three months given where you are right now is just about zero."

We referred her to a teacher whose class she joined. In her email Thank You note she told us that her husband appreciated the call with us because there was "no hype."

- We were specific and authoritative.

- We were grounded in our expertise, because we'd been where she was and knew what she needed.

- She was moved by our clarity and felt safe to trust our referral.

- She and her husband saw the benefits of our recommendation and followed it to the letter.

So when you want to say—"Are you nuts?"—make sure you look first at what you are doing. Or rather, what you are not doing. And then focus on how you're cheating yourself and your visitors of your most profound expertise.

#14. When creating soft sell marketing messages, which words reassure and establish relationship quickly? Which words push people away?

The trouble with your question is that you're asking for a formula, a predetermined set of words that you can plug in no matter what you're marketing or promoting. This approach has little or no connection to who you are and who your customers are. What you're asking for is a kind of robo-sales-copy. One size fits all. And that's not soft sell marketing.

This doesn't mean you can't use pre-written templates to get a start. They can help jog your creativity and get you beyond a blank page.

But depending on robo-sales-copy will never connect with your reader and establish a good relationship. Quite the contrary, robo-sales-copy is like a machine-generated drumbeat. Mechanical. Stiff. So exact as to lose all of the emotional excitement of being truly alive. Rather than draw people to you, robo-sales-copy will more than likely push people away—and they may not even know why. They'll just sense something isn't right.

Reassure Quickly

These two words---Reassure and Quickly---expose a less-then-sincere intent on your part.

What do you need to reassure your potential customers about? That all you're doing is trying to make a sale and you don't want them to know or feel that? That you're presenting one face but intending another?

And what about "quickly?"

Although there's love-at-first-sight, real ongoing love requires two people to get to know each other. Because lasting love takes time. As for a commercial relationship, it takes between three to nine contacts before most people will buy. That's a standard marketing rule.

Is it possible that someone will buy-at-first-sight? Sure. But if you want a long-term business, you'll need to build relationships—real relationships that are respectful and rewarding for both you and your customers. That doesn't happen quickly. But it does happen when you use heart-based sales copy that draws your readers to know, like, and trust you.

Power Words

There are a number of words that marketers call "power words," *free* being one of them. And they are effective.

If that's what you're after, place this exact phrase in your Google Tool Bar Search Function— "power words" + marketing—and you'll get pages and pages of power word sites in Google's Organic Listings column.

However, even with a list of power words and phrases you still have to write copy that sincerely and authentically expresses who you are and what you have to offer your readers. It's your genuine connection with your readers and customers that forms the basis for a long-term business and not just a quick sale.

From-the-Heart Copywriting

Finally, you may simply need to understand the craft of writing soft sell/soft topic sales copy.

Sincere copywriting takes knowledge and practice and the good news is that there are basic guidelines, basic structures, and basic elements that you can learn immediately.

Don't trade your love of and enthusiasm for what you do for a set of power words. That's an inauthentic way to approach marketing and copywriting. Vote instead for the legitimacy of your own heart and soul, your true commitment and willingness to reach out to your readers and give them your truth in your sales copy. If a power word becomes integral to what you're writing, by all means use it.

Persuasive copy is the heart and soul of successful marketing. Mastering it will turn your business into the profit generator you want it to be.

We can help you with this. Look at our "Soft Topic Copywriting Secrets" home study course (page 173) . We give you both the basics of solid and effective copywriting as well as examples and special bonuses to support your sincere, heart-based sales efforts.

#15. I'm a psychotherapist and counselor and soft sell marketing is definitely aligned with my practice. How can I effectively market my business to stand out to potential clients, draw them to my practice, and develop an initial rapport with them through my marketing?

There are three points in your question.

1) You want to stand out to your potential clients.

2) You want to draw them to you.

3) You want to develop rapport.

Standing Out

Positioning is the idea used in traditional marketing to represent standing out. It's been called a battle for mindspace, or a battle for top-of-mind.

In their classic book *Positioning*, traditional marketers Al Ries and Jack Trout write: "Positioning is not what you do to a product. Positioning is what you do to the mind of the prospect." They mean that you work to stake out an advantageous position in the potential customer's mind relative to your competition. Provided you do it well, you will also establish yourself in a precise position in the marketplace.

This approach isn't about understanding your customer's needs and wants with the intent of making an emotional, person-to-person bond. It's an instrumental strategy—mechanistic and without sincere regard for the customer.

In this mechanistic approach, what you want is a "spot" you can claim as your own embedded in your customer's mind. Through consistent messaging you strive to drive in your message as deeply as your positioning techniques will bring about.

For example: When You Think Soda, Think Coke.

Coca Cola's positioning strategy shoots for a conditioned, kneejerk response. The sole objective is to assure that people buy Coke to satisfy the deeply conditioned, unconscious tug.

Not Much Mind

Ries and Trout write this about the mind of the customer: "Not only does the human mind reject information which does not match its prior knowledge and experience, it doesn't have much prior knowledge and experience to work with."

When you characterize people, as well as the human mind itself, as deficient, you start with the premise that you've got little to work with. Given that, what do you have to do to "get through?"

Voila, the need for a hard sell approach.

Now it's true that to market well you must deeply know your client's needs and dilemmas. But since you are a psychotherapist the idea of staking out a "spot" in someone's mind runs counter to the whole point of therapy. So how do you attract clients?

Being Fully Present

The power and authority of your being fully present is the foundation for being an attractor to those who need what you offer. Part of being fully present requires that you are altogether clear about your specific type of service and what you can do for your clients. No confusion. No muddle. Boldly claimed. Simple and direct.

Then your potential clients have little difficulty knowing who you are and determining whether what you offer is right for them.

But that's only half of the process. How do you draw them to you?

Stand On and Stand Out

When you are fully present you have a vivid and emotionally intimate sense of relationship with your potential client. You not only appreciate the human-to-human, heart-to-heart connection (versus concept-to-concept), you know that, in a very real way, your client is you and you are your client.

You stand on your internal foundation, the bedrock of your marketing efforts, and from there you stand out in the marketplace.

To help you design your marketing approach, answer these questions:

- What is your specialty? What do you bring to your clients that no one else in your field does? In other words, why should they be attracted to you?

- What are the primary benefits your clients receive? Not merely the results you promise, but the very specific doing-business-with-you results that no one else can offer.

- What role does your client play in your professional relationship? That is, how do you perceive your client? And how does your client perceive you?

- Ask colleagues who refer to you, specifically "Why you?" How do their answers align with what you know about yourself? What surprises you? What delights you?

- How would you write about your services for a box ad in the yellow pages? Short and to the point. Not to publish but to clarify and simplify your marketing message.

Rapport

The rapport you seek flows seamlessly from the connection your marketing clarity brings. You won't have to work at it. The relationship is already in place by virtue of your client's attraction to your promotional materials. It will then be up to you to nurture it, more fully expressing who you are, and in that way reinforcing your client's wisdom in choosing you. The truth is, you've chosen each other.

Also, please know that marketing is an ongoing practice. Don't expect to nail it on the first try. And understand that you will want to keep refining your message as you grow and change. That way your commitment to your own excellence is permitted to deepen, as will your ability to promote your services with greater certainty, integrity, and authenticity.

#16. What gives me happiness is providing service with heart and integrity and my new site is based on that. However, it's not translating into the income I need and desire. How do I stay about service and stop the fear conversation in my head?

One of the dangers for anyone who wants to come from service is a belief deeply hidden in the cultural unconscious that claims service is about giving and business is about making money.

One way of testing the presence of this belief in you is to pay attention to what comes to mind when we say—"employees of a non-profit organization."

Most people do *not* imagine large salaries. In fact, quite the contrary. Non-profit and especially charity organizations are thought to be populated by workers who don't make much money at all.

Whether that's actually true or not is irrelevant. The impression is that they don't. Or, to put it another way, the image of being in service doesn't usually link with a lot of money.

So soft sell marketers, whose first impulse is to provide care and change lives, not only do not immediately think about making money, they often are resistant to the idea of making a lot of money—as though money somehow corrupts service. That's one source of the fear conversation in your head.

The Fear of Being Fabulous

There is another source and it's personal. We call it "The Fear of Being Fabulous™."

It means that, no matter what you tell yourself, you don't have internal permission to succeed financially. The proof is right there in your question. If you had permission you certainly wouldn't be up against the barrier you struggle with.

You have constructed money limits in your own psyche, and those limits restrict your freedom to make the money you "need and desire."

No amount of technical learning about marketing, copywriting, web design, or sales will be enough to overcome your lack of permission. That's an inside job. So . . .

> **First**—Pay attention to the images and thoughts that come to mind, and the feelings connected with them, when you think about making money from your website. What thoughts prohibit you from the money you want? What images derail your desire and set up blocks to your internal ambition? Catalogue them. Doing that will make them concrete and more accessible.

> **Second**—Please don't bite on the bait of positive thinking. If that would have worked for you you wouldn't be asking what you're asking. Positive thinking is often a distraction, an escape actually, from truly facing into what you have put in your way. Because positive thinking doesn't go deep enough to tap into the source of your lack of permission.

> **Third**—Trace your feelings, images, and thoughts to their source. You do that by not challenging what arises, no matter how bizarre it may seem to you. Allow your thoughts and images to teach you about your inner life and lead you closer and closer to the source of being stuck. Don't deny. Listen.

Because you know, unconsciously, that your ambitions are internally prohibited, you've got good reason to be fearful. You know, at the outset, that you won't get what you need because you don't have internal permission to receive what you want. So you have reason to be afraid.

However, when approached with respect and care, your fear is a true ally. It's asking you to pay attention to what you're feeling, because what you're feeling is a signal of what you are unconsciously committed to.

We urge you to make the decision to change so that you can open your mind and heart to your own conscious desires. Because only then can you sell and make money without selling out to your own internal blocks.

We created our 12-CD program designed specifically for this kind of internal struggle. It's called "Overcoming the Fear of Being Fabulous."

#17. How can I let go of my guilt about having radiant prosperity when others are suffering and I know they can't afford my fees?

First let's take a look at your guilt. Guilt about "having radiant prosperity when others are suffering" can only exist within the framework of your deeply held responsibility for other people's lives. And that sense of responsibility points to a kind of narcissistic presumption that you are in charge of everything, which, of course, you are not.

While we are all deeply interconnected spiritually, the fact is that each of us makes critical decisions that guide our unique lives. Certainly our family and cultural/religious backgrounds can have a major impact on those choices. But you are certainly not responsible for the choices that have led to the suffering others experience and their inability to afford your fees.

First—Please allow your intelligence and the calling of your soul to move you to respect that other people are responsible for their choices and the lifestyles they've arranged for themselves. Allow them their own lives, their choices and consequences.

Second—In marketing your business, you're not going to succeed if you imagine that everyone on the planet is a likely candidate for what you provide. That's inflated. You can't be all things to all people.

You must determine who you most want to work with—what intellectual, spiritual, social, and financial level of people best match who you are and what you provide. This is only fair to you, because you acknowledge and permit yourself to be as comfortable and competent as you can be interacting with your clients. This way they will receive the best of the benefits you provide.

Third—You are only responsible for what you can effect, what you can influence and change. Nothing more.

So please recognize and respect that, like all of us, you have limits. When you do, you can shape your business to serve those who will best advance and thrive due to your specific services or programs. That means you get to choose who you serve, not be at the mercy of whoever shows up.

Finally—It's not at all helpful to your clients, or to the world at large, for you to go without. The world needs you to be a role model of what is possible. In fact, the world needs far more role models of ordinary people who have created very successful lives. To help those who are struggling it's important that they see what it's like when someone is living a life fully expressing their excellence. That is a spiritually grounded gift you can provide to all who meet and know you.

So What About You?

What must you do to let go of your preoccupation with people who cannot enjoy the abundance you enjoy?

What must you do to take charge of and hold yourself responsible for only your limited realm of influence?

What must you do to better impact your sphere of influence by being a role model for what's possible when you express yourself fully?

#18. Could you talk more about the conflict that many feel around spirituality and money and how we can allow ourselves to receive abundance for the healing work we do in the world?

We've just addressed the guilt some soft sell marketers feel about making money. In answer to this question we focus on the fundamental importance that you understand where you are living—and that's on Planet Earth.

No matter how spiritual you may feel, no matter how much you strive for ever higher consciousness, the fact is that you live in a physical world where you require money and commercial exchange, even if only to feed yourself each day.

So in order to ground yourself in what it means to be both human and spiritual you need to "Give unto Caesar what is Cesar's and give unto God what is God's."

Yet, we've seen so many soft sell entrepreneurs struggle in their businesses because they attempt to stay true to the misguided idea that only the God side of this instruction should be acknowledged. They rob themselves of the freedom to charge appropriately for their services (avoiding "worldly greed"), prevent themselves from standing apart from their colleagues (only humility and modesty are allowed), and lack internal permission to acknowledge their true gifts (that would seem narcissistic and selfish).

So we urge you to reconsider what it means to be both spiritual and make money.

Gifts From Beyond

Each of us has been blessed with gifts that come from far beyond our own private invention. To deny the world of your gifts is the opposite of spiritual.

When you use your gifts to help others, that is the essence of Spirit In Action. When you charge appropriately for your gifts, you honor both the Godly gifts you have, and you honor your Caesarly need to support yourself—all the while requiring others to honor the value of what you provide by paying you. That way you live in the truth of the actual, real life you are living.

Selling Is Spiritual Service

We remind you that when done with care and respect, selling is always spiritual service, because you are a guide for others into a better life.

It's a disservice to you and to them if you fail to provide your healing work. And it's a major disservice to you and to them if you do not charge what you're worth in the world of commercial exchange.

Why?

Because, when you give your gifts away, you make of yourself a servant or slave, available for the taking. And you require nothing from the people who receive your gifts. They are allowed to take you for granted and, therefore, as research routinely indicates, they fail to value the power of the sacred life experience you've provided.

#19. I'm a professional life coach. My vision is to be a support to my clients by asking the right questions and providing introspective tools to help them find their life's purpose. This is not a tangible product. How do I market it so it will motivate prospective clients to seek my services?

First, we need to clear up the confusion about "tangible" products versus "intangible" services. Because this is a source of serious concern (and self-doubt) for many soft sell marketers.

Tending to believe that there is a significant difference between a non-tangible service and a tangible product, many care-givers and service providers rank a tangible product as superior to a service. And in so doing they dig themselves deeper and deeper into frustration because they then can't fully claim the value of what they do provide.

This tangible/intangible problem generally arises when they try to describe in their marketing materials what they do and what they offer.

Tangibility Is a Distraction

If you're concerned about the non-tangible quality of your service, we ask:

Can you directly touch, see, hear, smell, or taste compassion? What about the critical insights you provide your clients? What about the care you feel that serves as the core ingredient of the transformational coaching you practice that produces the results you help your clients achieve?

And your clients' lives really do change, don't they? That's tangible. So much so that your results can be measured in terms of their new behaviors and their reports of new life satisfaction. That's tangible. Focusing on the intangible nature of your service is really a distraction, isn't it? Because you do get results. That's a fact.

So, the better question is—"How do I make clear in my marketing the very tangible results my clients achieve through the coaching strategies I offer them?" This question prevents your backing away from the real value of what you offer. Answering this new question shifts your focus and re-frames your understanding of what you do and the benefits you can promise.

So Now, Let's Do That

What you offer is a method and practice of re-organizing your client's internal life. That makes you a tested and proven authority on the internal realm of consciousness and self-understanding. It's in that area of experience that you are expert—with results to show for it.

Your practice is both formalized—you use a specific technique that is applicable to all clients—and you have to be spontaneous in the approach you take with your individual clients, because each person is different. So your work is both general and very individual and personal.

While you ask valuable questions, your real skill is in your practiced ability to ask the right questions, listen carefully, spot the tangles in your clients' thinking and feeling, make those tangles clear and evident, and suggest practical solutions so your clients can make the necessary changes they hired you to help them achieve.

If what you also want is a tangible product, formalize your questions into a specific structure and put them into an audio, video, or text format. You can then sell them as CD, DVD, or PDF.

But don't lose sight of your real value. A concern over its intangible quality will only dilute the power and authority of what you do.

Testimonials

Along with communicating the general nature of your coaching style, your best marketing advantage is to have your clients speak for your expertise—in other words, providing testimonials. You don't want their testimonials to merely praise your work. That's not emotionally convincing for the person looking for what you promise.

You need proof of specific results. You need client testimonials about where they were when they began with you and where they are now. What life changes have resulted from working with you.

We know you may have ethical considerations with regard to asking for and using client testimonials. And there is a lot of misinformation about testimonials—how to get them, what they should say, and how to use them. That's why we created our special report "The Art of Effective Testimonials" especially for care-givers
(http://www.softtopiccopywritingsecrets.com/tat).

Feeling-Based Marketing

Because what you do is internal, your marketing has to be largely feeling-based, whether video, audio, or text. So your marketing message has to be invitational instead of instructive, emotionally involving instead of merely informative.

Your own emotional transparency is vital. Your potential clients must sense your care and concern, and they need to see your willingness to reveal yourself.

Regardless of the intellectual, proof-based quality of your message, your authenticity needs to be communicated through the emotion you infuse into your marketing messages.

And your clarity—knowing yourself and knowing your results so that you stand out clearly among other coaches in your field—will allow your prospective clients to identify the specific promise that you are offering and thereby identify with you.

Their motive to choose you is fundamentally based on the ease with which they can identify the match between their needs and your special focus, their concerns and the trust you elicit, and the ease they feel with you through your marketing messages.

Don't fall for the idea that because your real gifts aren't tangible you won't be able to successfully market them. That's a fallacy. Many, many, many people are looking for you and what you have. It's your job to allow them to clearly feel and understand just what that is.

#20. How do you show your passion and spirituality without appearing phoney or frightening to customers?

Although this question may seem too specific and only applicable to this writer, we chose to include it because it speaks to a concern that is far more widespread than you might think. The idea of coming across as phoney is one we've heard from many soft sell marketers.

This is not an issue about customers, as it appears. Instead it has everything to do with the writer's internal life—an internal life that is blocked and stunted by fear.

Where Did This Fear Come From?

While your fear didn't start with your current career, you've now got yourself self-consciously uptight about expressing your strong, confident marketing voice whether it's in your advertising, sales pages, emails, and perhaps during teleseminars, or speaking on stage.

What a horrible bind you're in. And we can only wonder where this idea came from. Because soul-based passion and spiritual connection are exhilarating and attractive to nearly everyone who would be interested in your soft sell services and products.

However, and this is a major however, if you're talking about being pushy or over the top, desperate to grab your potential customers by their virtual lapels and shake, shake, shake to get their attention and their money, well, then we can understand your concern.

Since this question was pressing enough for you to write, we have to assume that you fall into this latter category—at least to some degree.

Your Lack of Confidence

The issue isn't your sincere passion and spirituality, but your lack of confidence in who you are and what you do. And that's not a fatal flaw. Far from it.

It just means that you can benefit from online marketing as a spiritual teacher.

In this context, we have to ask you what is it about confidently writing or speaking to your customers regarding the value of what you do that scares *you*? Because in your question it's *your* fear speaking, not the fear of your customers. They're not actually involved. You're the one who's concerned about your passion and your spirituality.

- Were you raised to believe that you have to be humble and modest, never tooting your own horn?

- Did you grow up assuming that if you were intelligent and talented you'd be discovered so you don't need to, and therefore shouldn't, put yourself out in front of people to get noticed?

- Have you been afraid that people would call you conceited or cocky if you claimed your rightful place at "the front of the line"?

Whatever it is that's held you back from comfortably putting yourself forward with confidence and high visibility, we urge you to use your marketing efforts to challenge yourself and dig deeper into the source of your fear.

What to Do

1) When you write your sales copy, before you publish or post it, read it out loud. See how it feels to hear what you've written. If you sense that you're coming on too pushy, examine the fear that's pushing you to go over the top. Then search internally for a more sincere way to say the same thing. Rewrite and rewrite until you've found your deepest, most compelling marketing voice.

2) Then call a friend and read it to them. Get feedback on whether your passion and spirituality are coming through sincerely or have been warped by your fear. Use this feedback to help you again search for where you're trapped in limiting beliefs, scrunching your spontaneous exuberance for what you do and what you want your reader to know about what you do. Then rewrite some more.

3) Now send the copy to your friend and have that person read your copy to you. See how you feel as you listen to your own message. The important word here is *feel.*

Because when you can feel confident that your message is coming from your heart and from your soul, you have no need to be afraid of your customers' response—especially their potential fear.

And remember, this is a process. You're not going to turn your fear around overnight. But you can allow your soft sell marketing needs to teach you more and more about who you really are.

And that's a deeply spiritual gift far beyond the money you make.

#21. What is the one thing I can do that will have my business stand out from my competition when my product is the same as my competitors?

We addressed the issue of "standing out" in Question #15 from the perspective of positioning. That's an external perspective, all about controlling the mind of the customer. Now we'll look at standing out from within your internal mindset.

We start with identification. That's a word that's not used very often in marketing conversations. "Identification." Yet every sale made is based on identification. No identification, no sale.

What Does Identification Mean?

We hinted at this in Question #15 when we said:

> Part of being 'fully present' means that you are altogether clear about your specific type of service and what you can do for your clients. No confusion. No muddle. Boldly claimed. Simple and direct.

You communicate what you offer with such clarity that you are easily identifiable by your potential clients. They have little difficulty seeing you and knowing who you are and whether what you offer is right for them.

Making yourself clearly identifiable is your marketing half of the identification process. Identifying with you is your client's side.

How Does Identification Happen?

Identification happens when your potential customer sees themselves in you. They recognize their experience in what you are presenting. And in their recognition they see you as an extension of themselves. That occurs consciously—"Wow, that's what I think!"—or unconsciously—"This really feels good to me."

The emotional connection is made through identification.

A number of years ago, when we were promoting our first book *The New Intimacy: Discovering the Magic at the Heart of Your Differences* we sent a proposal to the television show The View. We described how the differences between two people, when handled consciously, can be a gold mine of rich psychological and spiritual treasure.

In the proposal, as an example of differences, we included one line that read: She Saves, He Spends.

Four words in a 500 word proposal.

Our proposal hit the segment producer's desk just when they were planning a show on that exact topic. Identification ensued.

We were them and they were us, and we were immediately booked for the first of our two appearances on The View.

Was timing involved? Sure. But timing alone would not have been solely responsible for the connection we made without the identification.

Only four words, but exact—She Saves, He Spends—leading the producers to identify with us as the precise solution to their need for the show.

That's how every sale is made, through the internal identification in which two parties see themselves in one another.

So how do you "stand out"? By being as precise as you can in describing who you are, where you come from, what you have to offer, what people who use your product or service will get, and how they will benefit. That's the marketing way to express your love for your customers.

This is not a mysterious process. It simply requires clarity in understanding who you are and clarity in expressing your identity and value to those who are looking for you.

One Final Point

You mention your competition and your competitors. Please understand—and this is a core understanding—that you have *no* competitors except for those you create in your own mind.

Are there others who market in your niche? Of course. But they are not you and you are not them.

In fact, in the whole history of our five billion year old universe, there never has been another you, nor will there ever be—no matter how long the planet exists.

When you get yourself into the idea of competition, here's the reality of what your considering:

> To compete is to strive for the same goal as someone else
> and that goal is available to ONLY one of you.

Even when you achieve the goal (the sale in this instance), you can never be certain you will do so the next time around, because your competition may claim the *only* available goal the next time. Inside that mindset you can never, *never* be secure.

When you use your imagination to conjure up competitors, you create opposition, struggle, and scarcity. In that context, you have to use hard sell tactics to win. And, as we said, you never really win, so what's the point?

Please take this to heart—there is no other you. So there is no competition.

Work to identify yourself precisely and thereby set up the pathway for identification to occur. That's how the sale is ultimately made—And The Only Way It Is Made.

And more so, that's how you can be successful with your success, instead of always looking over your shoulder to see who wants to take it away.

To support your unique excellence give yourself the gift of a "You Are A Miracle" screen saver.

(http://www.youareamiracle.net)

#22. How do I reconcile hype with my ethics and pursuit of wholeness. What do folks in this position do to overcome our dilemma?

First let's look at "hype." What is hype?

Hype means to go beyond, to represent things or situations as much greater or less, better or worse than they really are. When someone does that consciously it's undeniable that they intend some deception for the purpose of emotional manipulation. And in marketing the clear purpose of that manipulation is to over-hype emotions so a sale can be made.

You can find hype everywhere—in sales, politics, advertising, show business, the covers of magazines at the check out stand to say nothing of the tabloids whose whole marketing format is to create super-hype and trigger hyper-response.

The problem with hype is that it's manufactured. Because it extends beyond the reality of the product or situation, it's not truthful and therefore not real. And, at its core, it is wildly self-centered, treating the potential customer as a mere object to be exploited.

It'll Change Your Life?

At a business conference where we recently spoke we watched another speaker drive the audience to high intensity excitement so that at the end of his presentation they would buy his high-priced product at the back of the room. As a bonus to his product offer, he described the radio show he hosts and told the crowd that anyone who bought his offer that day would get to co-host a segment of his show. Then he claimed that their appearance on his show would "change your life," and that the financial value of this opportunity was $25,000!

Now, we've been on Oprah (Jim), The View, O'Reilly Factor (Judith), CNN, Canada AM, The Daily Buzz and many other television shows along with over a thousand radio shows. We anticipated our appearances would lead to massive book sales. But the fact is you're there to serve the needs of the show, not the other way around. And that only makes sense. So we now know, for a fact, that if the show host does not directly mention your product and directly endorse it, your sales will be minimal, and certainly far less than anything you might have imagined.

So hosting a segment of any kind of radio show is hardly going to "change your life." In fact, unless you are featured, your appearance won't be worth much more than a line in your bio. So the $25,000 claim is not just inflated, it's patently false.

But that's the kind of hype that people fall for every day and lose thousands and thousands of dollars hoping against hope that they will grab that gold ring on the merry-go-round.

Paint the Real Picture

So how do you market within your desire to live a life of integrity and wholeness? By sincerely, authentically, and directly telling people about the actual value you offer. To do that you have to understand the value deeply—not just in numbers, but in the genuine promise to meet the expectations of your buyers.

- If you've created the product or designed the service you know its features and benefits from your own experience, so you understand them first hand.

- If you're marketing someone else's product or service as an affiliate, be sure to know the reputation of the product producer, and, better yet, try it out yourself so your authority and authenticity will be unassailable.

When you deeply understand your product value you will possess the insight to clearly and simply paint the picture of what you offer and the picture of how your offer will benefit those who use it.

And don't be afraid of your passion for your offer. Passion is life and vitality. Hype pretends to be vital but, in fact, it's empty. Heart-felt passion connects. Hype only appears to connect.

If what you offer has real value you won't need to exaggerate and go beyond the reality of its promise. And the sincere regard you hold for yourself and your customer will keep you within the conscience you need to market assertively and enthusiastically without undermining your personal and spiritual intentions.

#23. Is curiosity a useful tactic for relationship selling?

How can you be assured of making a sale if you don't know what your prospective customer needs, wants, or is resistant to? How can you compose any effective message, be it email, audio or video text, or a sales page if you don't hold a sincere interest in how what your customer needs aligns with what you offer?

The death-stroke of many businesses is the assumption that what they offer will satisfy their customers without finding out first. We did that early on in our marketing enterprise and the shock when we were not met with acceptance was, well . . . shocking!

Curiosity Is Essential

Curiosity is absolutely essential to any kind of successful selling, and most especially to relationship-based selling. Without curiosity you are locked within the limits of your own view of what your prospective customers want and need, which may not, and almost by definition, will not be broad enough, inclusive enough, or on-point enough to be successful.

Okay, so now what?

As we've said, every successful sale is a co-creation between you and your buyer. It's an improvisation with you listening carefully as your prospective buyer tells you what he or she has in mind.

There's nothing new about listening. Tom Hopkins, master sales trainer, writes in his book *The Art of Selling,* "By not talking all the time, by listening most of the time . . . the true professional maintains a friendly attitude of interest and understanding . . ." and encourages prospective customers to reveal what they want, what they fear, what they dream of so the salesperson can help them fulfill their desires.

You can't do that without curiosity.

The Soft Sell Partnership

Adding to curiosity the understanding that the seller and buyer are true partners in the sale changes the whole dynamic. This relationship implies more, much more than a one-time sale controlled by the seller. It's grounded in the desire for a long term relationship between human beings rather than between marketer and customer, between sale and bottom line—the external elements of the process.

To get a sense of this, bring to mind someone you buy from on a regular basis. Maybe the person who cuts your hair. Or perhaps you've bought the same make car from the same salesperson at the same dealership for the past 10-15 years.

In our case, we consistently shop at our local Whole Foods Market; Office Max for stationery needs; Best Buy for tech needs; Postnet for everything from shipping to printing business cards

Why do we keep returning? Satisfaction is an obvious reason. But why are we satisfied? In large measure because the staff members at each of these stores are excellent at soft sell. Eager to help. Honest. And always friendly, recognizing and welcoming us. We never feel "pushed" into buying something. We never feel like our needs are ignored in favor of some "special of the day." So we keep going back, and back, and back.

When you look at the places you return to regularly, if you keep asking why, in the end you will see that you return because of the relationship, the kind of relationship that acknowledges who you are.

You may even return because the interaction is non-emotional and that's to your taste. You don't have to "bother with all that relationship stuff." So you have a relationship in the form of a minimally curious, non-emotional relationship—but it's the relationship nonetheless.

The Questions In This Book

The questions we're answering in this book stem from our deep and sincere curiosity about the marketing and sales needs of our fellow soft sell marketers. We used an AskDataBase survey and posted a question online—"What do you most want to know about soft sell marketing?" We wanted our prospective customers to tell us what they wanted to know. While there were quite a few surprises, we were impressed with the repetition of several themes—all of which we're covering here in *The Heart of Marketing*.

Our curiosity, and the results we discovered, gave us a deep and wide understanding of what our fellow soft sell marketers are looking for. So we're confident that what we're providing in these pages connects with you and what you want. And consequently, you can feel assured that your connection with us will be emotionally meaningful and financially beneficial for you.

That mutual assurance, that reciprocal affirmation, is the basis of the co-creative partnership we speak of.

Not Merely a Tactic

But curiosity won't work well, or at all, if it's merely a "tactic." Then it's only a device and emotionally insincere. And it should be no surprise that curiosity, when used as a manipulative tactic, creates an arm's length feel rather than a source of sincere connection.

So stay in emotional connection and be true to the meaning of relationship. Listen to hear what you don't yet know. Deepen your awareness of what your customers want and what your marketing message needs to be. And the payoff? Your next product or program will flow effortlessly from your idea to your customers' purchase.

When you want to survey your list members, we recommend the AskDatabase software program we use. You can get a $1.00, 21-Day Trial Membership by going to:

(http://www.softsellaskdatabase.com)

#24. Do you make use of "urgency" or "scarcity" in soft sell marketing?

Urgency and scarcity are two of the jewels in the hard sell crown. They are meant to motivate a prospective buyer to buy *now*. They are rooted in a perception that the customer either cannot or will not take action and buy without being driven to do so.

This perception leads to manufactured or contrived urgency and deliberate scarcity.

What's fascinating about both these tactics is that they arise out of a lack-mentality on the part of the marketer as well as the buyer.

Grounded in Loss

Scarcity and urgency are selling and buying tactics that arise from a sense of want—laced with fear and lack:

- Want on the part of the marketer to accumulate as much money as possible, and, without the message of scarcity to motivate the buyer, the marketer fears not reaching his or her financial goals;

- Want on the part of the buyer who, because of a believed scarcity, fears being left out of something special and is moved to act now in order to obtain whatever that something special is.

Both sides of the transaction operate from a sense of possible loss and deprivation.

Both sides focus on the external elements of the transaction—the goods or services that are either actually in short supply, or have been artificially limited to create scarcity and urgency.

The problem with contrived scarcity and urgency is that, arising out of a fundamental sense of lack, neither side can ever be truly satisfied. No matter how well a transaction goes, both are left wanting more. So there is a perpetual sense of hunger and danger.

Scarcity in the Soft Sell Transaction

When scarcity has an internal base it is organic and authentic. For example, we offer a 3-day program we call "Magnify Your Excellence." We work with participants to remove the internal, unconscious psychological blocks that stand in the way of their larger success in all areas of their lives. To make the weekend as effective as possible we allow only 30-50 people to attend. These are not arbitrary numbers. Given our 20-year experience leading workshops we know that we can't deliver the same quality if the group is too large.

Might we set the limit at 25? Sure. But we allow as many people to attend as possible—between 30 and 50 depending on the focus and the location—because we are also in business and want to generate as much income as we can while still delivering highest quality.

When scarcity is real, and a transaction goes well, there is little if any residual hunger. The chances increase that both seller and buyer will be satisfied.

Urgency in the Soft Sell Transaction

Urgency—authentic, internal urgency—has little to do with external factors. It arises, most powerfully, out of the intensity of the potential buyer's need. The more compelling the need, the more it requires immediate action. The more the individual feels pressured internally to find resolution, satisfaction, or healing, the more he or she will be motivated by actual and pressing urgency. So decisive action results from the intensity of the need actually felt.

For example, imagine that it's the middle of the night. You're suffering with a bad cold and you've run out of decongestant. You're coughing and your sinuses are stuffed and hurting. You'd like some relief but it's 3:20 AM. To get what you need means getting out of bed, dressing, and driving to a local 24-hour pharmacy.

How likely are you to get up and go?

Now imagine that it's 3:20 AM and your first child, 2 years old, has a fever of 103. You've tried everything you know and the temperature just won't come down.

How likely are you to go to the 24-hour pharmacy now?

When you understand the depth of your customer's need you can craft your sales presentation to both pinpoint their need as well as demonstrate how your solution will satisfy and eliminate that need.

Genuine urgency arises out of the actual felt intensity of need.

Authentic Rather Than Contrived

It's important that you understand the internal, motivating source and psychological ground of sincere urgency and scarcity. When you do, you'll place yourself in better connection with your customers. You will love them for who they are and they will love you back with their loyalty and further purchases.

We stress the use of sincere and authentic scarcity and urgency because marketing with consciousness and conscience is more than just our slogan, it is the framework for successful soft sell marketing.

#25. How do you "sell" healing when you don't want to falsely raise hopes?

We offer our respect for you and all soft sell marketers—and marketers of every stripe—who are concerned about honesty and integrity and not misleading potential customers. As we said at the start of this book, for too long marketing and sales have had a bad reputation, because people in general have viewed being sold as the equivalent of stepping into a trap. Thankfully that's beginning to change, largely due to those marketers whose intention is to offer help—first and foremost—rather than simply going after more and more money no matter what it takes.

"Sell" Healing?

First, you can't "sell" healing. Although a money transaction is necessary for many reasons, the idea that you have to "sell healing" guts the value and promise of selling and of healing.

But you can point to the results you've seen your clients achieve after using your protocol and make certain that your prospective clients are clearly aware of those results.

The Issue of Raising False Hopes

You are an expert in your field. More important, you're viewed by your potential clients as an expert. Because they need your services, and in some cases desperately need your services, they will bestow on what you say more than you might intend. You can't avoid that. Their interpretation arises out of the urgency of their need. The more urgent, the greater your perceived or expected powers.

At the same time, as an expert, you are responsible for helping them imagine the future they want by showing them the healing outcomes your clients have already achieved.

That's the balance you must strike: showing prospective clients what is possible yet knowing full well they may bestow more onto what you are saying than you intend.

This is where the truth comes in.

Vigilant in Disciplining Yourself

For your sake as well as your clients', you must be vigilant in disciplining yourself with regard to what you say in your advertising and promotion. You know well that any real healing results from you and your client working together as a team.

You provide the specific recommendations of your protocol. You lay out all the various ways you supply support. You detail the responsibilities you expect from your client and from yourself in the collaboration.

And then you must stress that you cannot help anyone who won't help themselves. Your clients are fully responsible for their participation. You must help your clients remain rooted in reality, because it's only in reality that the results you both want can be experienced.

Your concern about "false hopes" is understandable in a culture where hype and spin are taken for granted. But you won't engender false hopes when you adopt and practice a policy of honesty and truthfulness on your side, and by asking questions of your clients to determine how they are interpreting the process between you.

The benefit to you of your ongoing inquiry is that your sincere and watchful concern is a sign of your genuine care—and a solid marketing practice.

Finally, What About the Truth?

Sadly, the world of advertising and marketing presumes that people don't want the truth, that they won't buy if all they have is the truth. They must be "motivated" and the truth is a downer.

But the replacement of truth with hype and nonsense sends people running to the refrigerator during television commercials, flipping past the ads in magazines, and tossing direct mail in the trash unread.

Ultimately hype is not and cannot be satisfying. Quite the contrary. It's disappointing and disheartening because it's not real.

Genuine truth is truly satisfying, because only the truth can be trusted. Only the truth yields the real results your clients are looking for. So when you tell the truth about your offer and the actual evidence of what is possible for them, you not only love your buyers by meeting them at the heart of their deepest need, you also protect yourself from playing yourself down or hyping what you have, and in either case, selling yourself out.

#26. How do I overcome my fear of being rejected when people don't buy my products?

When we first began marketing and people didn't buy what we expected them to, we certainly felt feelings of rejection. We imagined that they judged what we were offering as unacceptable, unsatisfactory, or useless. That really hurt. But since we really had no idea why potential customers were not buying, we were the ones who were making those hurtful judgments.

That prompted us to take a closer look at what they were really telling us.

While we have compassion for your feelings of rejection, it's important that you look at a deeper stream of difficulty floating below the surface of your fear of rejection.

Fear of Rejection

One of the major, if not *the* major challenge for all of us who market our own products and services is a conscious or unconscious fear of rejection—followed by misinterpreting our potential customers' behaviors as rejection—whether they are or not.

When people don't buy, there are two major considerations:

1) There isn't a good fit between what you're providing and the person who's visiting your site. That happens.

But when you're caught in the fear of rejection, everything becomes personal. The visitor's choice becomes your fault. There *must* be something wrong with the way you're doing things. You berate yourself under the pressure of believing that they had an interest—albeit minimal—or they wouldn't have stopped at your site. And you were unable to sell them. So it's you. It must be you. You're inept, maybe even incompetent.

If that's what you go through, we understand. However, sometimes you simply have to accept that what you are providing in the marketplace just won't work for your visitors. More important, you can't sell everybody. That illusion is the source of the mental and emotional thrashing that so many naive marketers suffer.

To repeat—sometimes what you have isn't a good fit with what people are looking for.

You know that's true because you've had the experience of leaving a website or walking away from a sale because the product or service just didn't fit for you.

2) You may not be marketing well. If that's the case:

- You're not making yourself and your product/service clearly visible and distinctly identifiable.

- You haven't painted an engaging picture of the results—and the benefits of the results—your customer can anticipate.

- You haven't uncovered what your prospective customers actually need, let alone what they want.

- You aren't sufficiently immersed in the details of your offer to interest them, let alone capture your potential customers' attention and energize their expectations.

Different from the first consideration when there really isn't a good fit, in this case the issue does come back to you—you as a marketer.

What's the Real Issue?

Your fear of rejection is causing you to hang back, to distance yourself instead of becoming completely and wholeheartedly involved. It's a self-perpetuating cycle that, if not turned around, will cycle you right out of business.

But here's the good news. You can change.

You will require an internal as well as an external change. And this needed change is not beyond your reach. We call the internal aspect Overcoming the Fear of Being Fabulous. Couple this with learning solid marketing principles and practices from qualified and competent mentors—the external aspect.

We Keep Reminding . . .

That's why we keep reminding ourselves and reminding you—our fellow soft sell marketers—that selling is spiritual service and that Internet marketing is a spiritual teacher. We want you to have a deeper and deeper grasp on the many ways business confronts us all with a larger reality than we're typically used to.

One of the supreme blessings of being in business and facing into the demands of marketing is that there's no way you can sell out when you run your business with consciousness and conscience. Each challenge is an opportunity to grow yourself larger, improve your marketing skills, take bolder actions, and conquer the doubts that have delayed your larger success until now.

#27. How do I sell without making a nuisance of myself?

Somehow, like so many of us, you learned to associate selling with being a "nuisance." Rather than filled with conviction and confidence that you are providing valuable service to those who need and want what you offer, you're convinced that your sales efforts are annoying, intrusive, and worse yet—unwanted.

But where does this come from?

Millions of sales people around the world are happy to share their expertise and advice selling anything from hardware to lingerie, baby formula to breath mints. Yet when you, as a care giver, a soft sell marketer, put yourself forward in the marketplace you are saddled with an inner gnawing, a voice that whispers in the night that you're doing something wrong.

And you find yourself trapped within your own sense of social conscience—because there is a lack of balance between your care-giving heart and your innate feeling of responsibility for others. Your self-regard is nearly trampled by guilt and fear should you be putting forth anything that feels like self-interest.

So you feel like a nuisance, sometimes a super-huge nuisance.

Obama and McCain

While writing this book, the Obama/McCain presidential campaigns were the marketing event of our times. Did either of the candidates feel like a nuisance when they spoke to their crowds? Hardly.

In fact, each of them knew that he had the vision for what the majority of his followers wanted. They knew to market themselves from the platform that best fit the needs of their respective voters. Now, while you may not think of the presidential electoral process as marketing, that's what it is—marketing.

And that's what you are doing. The same thing presidential candidates do. Marketing.

The question is, how can you become as clear as the candidates in providing exactly what your prospective buyers want?

About Making a Nuisance of Yourself

The only way you can make a nuisance of yourself is to thrust your message in front of people who do not want to hear it. Obama and McCain were in front of people every day for nearly two years. Almost all of them wanted what their candidate was offering.

Could they have been a nuisance? Only if they were barging in on the opposing candidate's events, going where they were not wanted. Only then would either of them have been a nuisance.

You can never be a nuisance when you speak with respect and care to those who want what you offer.

Never a Nuisance When . . .

- You're never a nuisance when you are called to service.

In Question #9 we talked about a soul-based business. As we said, when you touch your deepest personal truth, you discover just how perfectly your offer resolves the needs of those in your specific audience; you have a deep sense of the powerful benefit of your business to your customers and to you; and what you bring to the market is not arbitrary, not sold just for the money, but arises out of your connectedness with your specific audience.

There is a sense that you are called to service. You have no choice. What you discover is what you *must* do as a business person. And when you follow that call, there is no way you can be a nuisance, because for those who are looking for you, you can't be either offensive or annoying.

- You're never a nuisance when you provide what your customers want.

It goes without saying that you must provide information that your customers find useful, whether it's no-cost or for a fee.

Obama and McCain delivered their messages to audiences giving them hope and support and a sense of belief and belonging.

How can your messages, your services and/or products provide the hope your customers are looking for? How can you make your messages the embodiment of joyous, generous interaction, knowing that those who need what you're selling will eventually buy?

- You're never a nuisance when you teach your list members what to expect.

Gauge the timing of your email contacts according to what you've led your customers to expect.

Some marketers email their list members six days a week, every week, all year long. Two major soft sell marketers come to mind. They are successful because that's what their followers expect and want.

Other marketers only mail out 1-2 times a week providing sufficient contact and connection for their needs and the needs of their list members.

One marketer we know mails out only once a month. Every time we receive her email we're surprised and realize we haven't known whether or not she was still in business—because she's so nearly invisible.

Remember, if you are sincerely offering a solution to a problem, you are not an inconvenience, you are not a disturbance, you are not troublesome, nor disruptive. Quite the contrary, you are a benefit, and, depending on the urgency of your customer's need, you are a relief, maybe even a blessing.

#28. What is the biggest stumbling block in reaching customers when you are trying to "get the message out" with a spiritually-based soft sell topic?

Whether you are marketing a spiritually-based topic or anything else, the major stumbling block you'll encounter boils down to your reluctance to fully and confidently believe in and trust the marketing process. And it's clear from your question that this is an issue for you.

By saying that you are "trying to get the message out" your language exposes your unconscious resistance to being more assertive in your marketing—and therefore successful.

No Such Thing as Trying

First, there's no such thing as "trying." You are either getting your message out or you're not. When you say you are trying, you're not looking directly at what you are actually doing.

So whatever you're doing, whatever actions you are taking are successfully resulting in *not* getting your message out.

You have to face into what you *are* doing and own that the results you are getting are precisely, albeit unconsciously, the results you want. Otherwise you would be doing something different. This may be a little hard to swallow. But to make progress you have to start with where you actually are.

Is It Your Message?

Look at how you characterize your message, because you're unconsciously avoiding a personal stake in it. Why? Because you describe your message as "the message." Three letters that keep you at an emotional arm's length, and you thereby reduce the attraction power of what you're doing.

So we can't help but wonder what else you're doing to keep yourself from fully and confidently believing in and trusting your marketing process.

Marketing vs Publicity

Another stumbling block arises when people think they're marketing but all they're doing is generating publicity by putting up a website, or passing out business cards, or scheduling an appearance on a radio show or in a newspaper, or running an ad in a magazine or online ezine.

While each of these publicity elements can be part of your marketing plan, unless you know how and are willing to stand apart from the crowd in your particular niche—standing tall, proud, and persuasive— no one will be able to see what's unique about who you are and what you do, much less feel the message that will move them to buy from you.

What we're talking about is your unconscious resistance to marketing— marketing with the solid intention of reaching the widest audience with the largest message, moving the greatest number of people to become customers.

Major Causes

This unconscious resistance to being fully involved, which is nearly epidemic among soft sell marketers, stems from a number of major sources:

- Ignorance about tested and proven marketing and sales techniques;

- Lack of self-confidence which creates half-hearted effort;

- False humility used to praise yourself as virtuous when what you're doing is hiding;

- Doubting the value of your service or product which prevents you from being wholehearted in the actions you take;

- Lack of clarity about your offer which prevents you from allowing who you are to be seen, and that's a sure way to end up merely "trying to get the message out."

With regard to the first category, "Ignorance about marketing and sales," this is a mechanical problem and fairly easy to resolve. You need to study the principles of effective marketing and sales and apply them. And you're learning many of them—from a soft sell perspective—in this book.

The remaining categories all result from an inner prohibition against expressing your magnificence—the major stumbling block in the way of getting out your marketing message.

Soft sell marketers have the most difficulty with this because we are committed to not tooting our own horns. But toot you must if you're going to attract the attention of those people who are looking to find you among the clamor of all those providing services and products in your particular niche.

You owe it to yourself and your marketing success to find out how you can lay open the root of what's holding you back, and ensure it will never happen again.

That's the purpose and the promise of our program "Overcoming the Fear of Being Fabulous."

#29. How can speaking my truth from my heart allow me to make megabucks?

"Megabucks" is a term for wealth largely associated with the lottery, so we're curious about your use of it here. It's almost as if you're not permitted to say "tremendous wealth," "great wealth," or "millions every year."

To get a feel for what we're talking about, read these phrases out loud:

- How can speaking my truth from my heart allow me to make megabucks?

- How can speaking my truth from my heart allow me to make tremendous wealth?

- How can speaking my truth from my heart allow me to make great wealth?

- How can speaking my truth from my heart allow me to make millions every year?

- How can speaking my truth from my heart allow me to make megabucks?

Megabucks falls pretty flat, almost tinny when said out loud, especially after repeating the phrase "millions every year." Using "megabucks" lets you hide and never have to look directly at your desire to create wealth.

Soft Sellers' Shyness About Wealth

We're not surprised that the person who sent in this question appears to have a difficult time taking wealth seriously. For too long most care-

115

givers—whether massage therapists, midwives, parenting counselors, or piano teachers—have experienced themselves as servants to the needs of others. Their ethics, whether professional or personal, have prohibited the goal of amassing great wealth "at the expense of others."

We've struggled with it too. And sometimes still do.

So if you find it at all difficult to envision great personal wealth coming from the work you do, we want to support you in examining the conflict between what it feels like to speak your core business truth straight from the heart and then imagine great wealth coming from precisely that source. Then we encourage you to go beyond imagining. Speak your desire, your commitment to creating wealth. Speak it out loud—to yourself at first and then to others, bearing witness to your very real desire.

Become comfortable with what great wealth will feel like: • what you will do with it; • how others will respond to you because you possess it; • what you and others will think of you after you amass it. These are serious questions that using "megabucks" as a substitute will never address. In short, don't back away from the wealth you want.

Can Truth Equal Money?

Today we enjoyed phone calls with two trusted friends and colleagues that brought us invaluable soft sell marketing ideas for our Soft Sell Marketers Association—ideas that resonated with the truth of who we are as well as true for our specific marketing purposes.

In neither case were we paying for professional consultation. But if we had been, these new marketing ideas would each have been worth several thousand dollars for the profit that they will, in due time, generate for us.

So truth can equal money. And big truths can equal big money— perhaps millions every year.

That's why we want to help you ground yourself in the value of your truth, so that you can speak your truth from your heart, value that truth in the commercial market, charge accordingly, and create whatever wealth you desire.

Your Truth Changes People's Lives

In contrast to hard sell, money-to-money exchanges where the hoped for outcome is more money for everyone involved, in your soft sell business your truths can deeply change people's lives. And that can be invaluable whether it's improved health, better interview skills, greater romance, easier dog training, smart dating for frustrated singles, you name it. There's no limit to the lifelong value that your truth and your wisdom can provide.

Truth, genuine truth, is solid, trustworthy, emotionally touching, and opens the doors to the future in ways that clever techniques and superficial advice never can.

So your truth is worth money. Substantial money.

- Can you ask for it?

- Can you collect it?

- Can you deposit it into your sense of personal worth?

- Do you value the power of your truth as the key to creating your future wealth?

- Can you now take wealth building seriously?

Important questions with even more important answers.

When you are a Gold Member of our Soft Sell Marketers Association, we support you in knowing that your truth is your most abundant source of wealth.

#30. How can you close a sale without pushing too far?

You imply in your question that closing a sale requires some pushing. Otherwise you wouldn't be concerned with pushing "too far."

Why would you have to push too far? Why would you have to push at all?

To better respond to your question we need to look more closely at the difference between the external and internal elements of marketing and selling, the difference between "closing the sale" and "opening the relationship."

Perception of Your Potential Customer

How you perceive your customer is the source of your belief that pushing is necessary—even though you don't want to push, at least not too far.

Just as in Question #24 about urgency and scarcity, the idea of pushing to close the sale also comes out of an attitude of scarcity. Your customer is perceived as lacking the willingness or commitment to go forward and that necessitates your need to push.

So then the customer is to blame. And because of their perceived apathy, indecisiveness, ignorance, fear, or whatever—they are at fault. If they'd change all would go well. They won't so they need to be pushed—at least that's been the underlying belief for decades. But it's overdue to re-think this, because this belief creates an adversarial relationship rather than one that is helpful and collaborative.

Resent Being Pushed

Soft sell customers resist and resent being pushed. Why? Because a pushy sales pitch—and here we consciously and pointedly use the word "pitch"—is not about them but about you, the marketer/seller.

If someone has to be pushed then, by default, they either haven't been convinced or don't want the product or service to begin with. So the "push" is all about closing the sale from the marketer's needy and one-sided point of view.

> **Jim:** When I briefly worked as a retail salesperson I was told—"Once they walk out the door they're gone. The chance of their coming back is practically nill."
>
> I was told I had to "close them" before "they got away."
>
> I wasn't very good at it, though I tried, and I didn't last very long. I watched the other salesmen do whatever it took to close the sale—and more often than not "what it took" was not very respectful of the customer.

Lay Out Your Case Clearly

Each customer has his or her own degree of interest based on their degree of need. Not everybody who sees your offer has a need for it, or at least not an immediate need, so they are not candidates to buy. But for all those who might, you must lay out your case for the value of your offer—what it does and how the buyer will benefit—as clearly and persuasively as possible.

We encourage you to carefully answer these questions so you can clearly lay out your case:

- What problem is your customer wrestling with?
- How does the problem impact their life?
- Why can't they solve the problem on their own?
- What are the choices they've already made that are not working?
- Why should they listen to you? What is your solution?

- What are the benefits that result from your solution?
- What have your previous customers reported about the success of your solution?
- What other proof do you have for the effectiveness and value of your solution?
- What will their future be like after they've applied your solution and it's worked?
- What will they lose if they don't choose your solution?
- What guarantee do you offer to redirect the risk back to you?
- What is the spiritual value of your solution?
- What integrity do you bring to your offer?
- What credential and/or life experience do you possess to make yours a valid offer?
- How can you demonstrate your solution and the effects your customers will experience?
- And in what ways do you love your customers?

To fully open the relationship, you must paint the picture of what your customer's life will be like after they've used what you have for them. That speaks directly to the intensity of their need and connects with the organic urgency they're already experiencing.

You can do this with complete integrity because you know what your offer can do for them. That's not pushy. That's loving and it's good sales.

#31. How do I train my brain to realize it's ok to ask for the sale because what I am offering is of value to them, and not just money to me?

We know that many sales coaches, especially those with a hard sell orientation, typically focus on training the brain. But it's not your brain you need to focus on. It's your heart. We'll get back to this in a moment, but first . . .

Helpers and Money

We've referred to the principle—"Give unto Caesar what is Caesar's and give unto God what is God's." By this we mean that our lives on this planet are made up of the mundane—Caesar's world—and the transcendent—God's dominion. Yet we've seen so many soft sell people struggle in their businesses because, as we've said, they attempt to stay true to the misguided idea that only the God side should be acknowledged.

These folks struggle because they don't really have their feet on the ground. They struggle against not only being in the world but being of it.

When you aren't grounded here on planet Earth with a clear sense of your value to others, or when you're worried about indulging in "worldly need and greed," you rob yourself of the ability to charge appropriately for your services.

Being a Model

If you don't see yourself as being of this world with permission to ask for the sale, what kind of model are you being for those you serve? Do you want your children or your clients to struggle between the conflicting intentions of providing value for others and wanting to be compensated for their value?

Emotionally many service providers are afraid of "selfish, greedy guilt" for considering their own needs on a par with the needs of their clients. To avoid the guilt they back away from asking for what they want and then wrestle with their own negative head talk that blasts at them for not asserting their rightful value in their own eyes as well to their potential customers.

Other-Focused

Care-givers and service providers are characterologically other-focused. Their sense of identity and success is intimately entwined with the success and well-being of their clients and customers. So when they have to ask for the sale or payment for services and/or products and thereby are compelled to shift their focus to themselves and their own needs, they then struggle with an almost knee-jerk discomfort.

For example, have you ever wondered why, after you see the doctor, you're always sent to the office staff to be told what you will be charged? The doctor may say that this protocol frees him or her to focus on doctoring. But we've been told by more than a few doctors that money collection is too uncomfortable for them and they claim it "would ruin the doctor-patient relationship." So they hand the task of money collection over to a staff member.

We encourage you to heal this split and support both God and Caesar—both your client's needs and your own. And the first step toward healing the divide is your sincere and committed acceptance of where you live—here on Earth where commerce (i.e. money) and care (i.e. love) can and need to co-exist.

Then what follows is the progressive integration of both money and love. Then your desire for money and love can be turned into a coherent, whole intention to serve others as you serve yourself.

If you avoid this, your experience will be fragmented—leaving the ROI hard-sell marketers to accumulate more and more money, while you, as an ROE soft sell marketer, provide valuable and needed services yet struggle financially. No matter your spiritual beliefs, this result can't be one you would recommend to others and applaud them when they "achieve" it. So we urge you not to live under this burden for yourself.

Your Brain Will Follow Your Heart

You know that what you offer is of value. You know that what you offer is needed. And you've had clients express their gratitude for what you've given them. So your value is not the issue.

For you, as for many soft sell marketers, it's about coming to terms with being in Caesar's world. You know about God's dominion—whatever you understand God to be. It's Caesar's world that you must love with as much of your heart as you do the well-being of your clients.

You must love your Self, that Self that lives in this world—and the fact that you have worldly needs just like everyone else. You must accept and love the fact that you have respectable worldly ambitions that have supported you becoming the care-giving soft sell marketer that you are.

You not only have the right to ask for the sale, your care-giving job is not complete until you do. Because the payment from your client/customer completes the circle, making sure your client or customer gives back to you.

When you love your customer you must allow them to love you back.

#32. What is your view on how to attract customers via the internet vs. "getting" customers? Seems like there is a fine line there, especially when you cannot meet people in person.

It's true that the power of someone's physical presence tends to be more of an attractor than relating through email or an online sales page. But you've also had the experience of being in the presence of people who were not magnetic or charismatic. For whatever reason, their physical proximity wasn't an asset.

So attraction isn't about just being in someone's physical presence. It has to do with the inner qualities of a person or the power of a particular message that those qualities express. If the person or the message is magnetic then attraction will happen. If not, not.

Getting

Now it's safe to say that you, like most people, have an intuitive understanding of the difference between "attracting" customers and "getting" customers, but let's make it explicit.

There's an implication in "getting" customers that you have to compel people to move in your direction. You believe they will resist your attempts to attract them so you have to chase them—not unlike "getting" a herd to move into a corral or pen.

Once you've "got" them the presumption is that they are available for your use—in the case of marketing and selling—for your income and profit.

"Getting" doesn't suggest that your customers, once you've got them, are then free to behave however they wish. The point of getting them is so that they will buy. In fact, some hard sell persuaders claim they can get people to buy whether they like it nor not.

From this mindset, the bottom line is that you have to effort to "get them" to move—otherwise they won't.

Attracting

"Attracting" has a completely different feel. To attract someone means that they see in you something that appeals to, fascinates, or intrigues them and they move toward you of their own accord. You're not chasing. You are a beacon, appealing to them, drawing them toward you.

And you are never penning them in. They are always free to go or stay.

They remain people in their own right with whom you have a mutually beneficial relationship and not objects whose sole purpose is to fulfill your income and profit ambitions.

The "getting" marketer is far less concerned with the "person in the customer" than the "customer in the person," and very much concerned with the money to be made.

Soft sell, "attraction" marketers place, as their highest priority, the person in the customer as they work together, in partnership, for the mutual benefit of both.

Attraction Marketing

To attract means to draw to yourself by being appealing. Your branding, publicity, and/or promotional messages stimulate if not excite emotions, thoughts, a sense of spirituality, or materiality—either one or all. Attraction is inviting rather than compelling. You become a beacon rather than a search light.

To be attractive means you possess some quality that captures the attention and involvement of those who are interested in who you are and what you offer.

Since attraction marketing is more about serving than selling—without losing sight that selling is, after all, the ultimate goal—your job is to make what you offer as attractive and attention-holding as possible. So it's how you go about the selling—placing service as your number one priority—with, as we've said, selling as a second but equal intention.

Think about service and what contribution you want to make to the lives of your clients and customers. To do that you need to clearly know who you are and the ultimate benefits of what you offer as well as what your specific audience needs and wants. And then you craft your branding and your commercial message in a way that makes you irresistibly attractive to those who are looking for you.

How to Begin

1) Begin by standing squarely within your own expertise. Being a true expert is very attractive to those who are looking for a solution to a problem they can't solve themselves. And you not only have a solution but you're an expert in your area. Let yourself shine through your marketing materials—emails, branding or home pages, sales pages, blogs, audios, vidoes, everything you use to place yourself in front of your specific audience.

2) Be sincerely of service. Don't prattle prop lines like "How can I serve you?" if you don't mean it. People will sense your fraudulence and, rather than come toward you, they will flee. When you keep in mind what your potential customers are looking for, your intention and your goal is to put forth information that will attract them. Attracting them through servicing their wants and needs is the center point of your marketing.

3) Do what you enjoy. Offer solutions you are passionate about. Your brightness will itself be an attractor.

4) When someone is in the middle of a problem, they can't see beyond it. So paint clear pictures of what your customers will receive from you and what they'll experience after they apply what you offer. It's your job

as an attractor to show them what is possible in vivid detail and help them open their minds to what it will be like on the other side of their current state of being.

5) Understand your customers deeply. That way, when they hear your message, they will know, intellectually and emotionally, that you truly do get where they are and you will be seen as trustworthy.

6) Stay in touch with your customers. Don't make a sale and then not communicate with them until you need another sale. Build a relationship and maintain it.

7) Make yourself emotionally, intellectually, and spiritually open to your customers. Not as a technique. Not as a gimmick. That approach, by default, is not open. Be a model for who you want them to be.

8) You need to attract through revealing who you are, clearly and distinctly, so that you are visible and readily identifiable to those who are looking for what you offer. When you are clear, you won't distract your potential customers with irrelevant verbiage as they work to figure out what you are trying to say. In other words, talk to them, don't pitch them.

9) Finally, as an attraction marketer you have the comfort of knowing that people who come to you are doing so of their own choice. They are self-selecting you as the product or service provider they want to do business with. That means they are a very good fit for who you are and what you have to offer. And they are more highly qualified and more likely to buy.

So there's no waste of time or effort—yours or theirs—when you practice attraction marketing. And as an attraction marketer you won't be just making sales. You will be attracting and then creating long-term customers.

As Mahatma Gandhi taught, "Be the change you want to see in the world." Be that for your customers.

#33. What is the best way to accurately determine what my ideal client's real perceived needs and wants are without doing an extensive survey?

You probably have the least expensive and effort-free "survey" right close by. It's you.

Because if you are a soft sell marketer chances are you provide products and services that you've developed within your own area(s) of personal or professional expertise, creating or discovering solutions for core problems.

That means you've gone through some type of personal ordeal or professional predicament that prompted you to find the solution you needed in order to make it through. And now you're offering your solution to others who have the same need or want.

No Survey - At Least to Start

Emotionally you know what it was like to need the solution you've invented or discovered. You know the frustration when you were struggling before you found the way out. You know what it's like to be looking for a product or service in the maize of all the products and services offered on and offline.

So you are already identified with your customer, because you've experienced his or her need. You already have your half of the emotional connection from which the ultimate sale will emerge.

You know the problem to be solved. You know the feelings. In short—you are your customer. So you don't have to do an extensive survey—at least to start.

Your Story

Sharing your personal story, which is also the story of the solution you've discovered and turned into a product or service, is the most powerful marketing technique you can employ.

- Tell your story directly and sincerely.

- Make yourself visible and clear, and . . .

- You will attract those who identify with the circumstances as well as the solution you now provide.

You'll need to learn the techniques of attracting potential customers, otherwise known as drawing traffic (to your website or store). And there are important and essential copywriting techniques that will help you make your presentation clear and compelling. But the core of your message is what you've gone through and how you overcame the obstacles that were in your way.

Our Story of Romantic Frustration

As we've told you, we are the best-selling authors of five books on romantic relationships. We've heard from many men and women around the world telling us how our books have changed their lives. Why? Because our books provide down-to-earth, real-life solutions to the day-to-day issues that arise in every relationship—including communication, intimacy, conflict, care, affection, and more.

In order to write from a level of deep understanding, what were the internal blocks we had to overcome?

> **Judith:** I began dating when I was fourteen and didn't marry until I married Jim when I was 44. I had dated for 30 years. All that time I kept wondering and eventually agonizing over why I wasn't married. What was I doing

wrong? What was wrong with me? I read book after book, went to workshops and seminars, and nothing changed.

Now Jim and I are happily married and have a relationship people respect and admire.

Jim: I was divorced twice before Judith and I met, and prior to our relationship I kept moving from relationship to relationship. I was serious in each one, but not until I met Judith did everything come together to experience a true romantic partnership. Together we delved deeply into the power and beauty of the differences between two people, and that has served as the foundation for our marriage.

Our books are the outcome of what we learned about our own difficulties with differences, and what we had to learn together to make our marriage work.

Judith knows the frustration of not being married and Jim knows the disappointment of not being able to keep a marriage together. Do you think there are men and women who would like to know what we discovered? Do you think we can relate to them and attract them to us? Of course.

Assess Your Story

Once you decide what product or service you are offering, or even if you're already marketing multiple programs, take the time to assess your story—emotionally, intellectually, and spiritually:

- What were the challenges you faced that your potential customers are facing now?

- What were your thoughts and feelings as you faced your challenges?

- What were the blindspots you had to bring consciousness to?

- How did you do that?

- How did you overcome your ego's resistance to change?

- What techniques did you use to achieve the well-being you now experience?

- In what ways did you have to change?

- Once you knew what you had to change, how did you do that?

- What kind of help did you need to accomplish the change you were after?

- How long did it take you to get to where you wanted to go?

- What were the principal behaviors you had to examine and change?

- What unconscious beliefs held you captive?

- How did you finally solve the problem you were facing?

- What benefits do you now enjoy after you made the change?

- What kind of support did you need?

- How did you have to re-assess your relationships, or your work, or your health, etc?

Answering these questions and as many more as you can imagine will set the foundation for how you will write and speak about your offer so that you can appeal to those who are looking for your solution, wanting to enjoy the benefits that you now enjoy.

Your emotional openness and clarity express the love you have for your customers. Their identification with you, demonstrated by their purchase of your product, expresses how they love you back.

#34. Will people who are used to hard sell marketing actually buy from soft sell marketers or will they not even notice the "buy" possibility because it's too "soft"?

When you suggest that people might not even notice the "buy" possibility because it's too "soft," it sounds like you imagine that soft sell marketing prohibits you from making strong and persuasive presentations.

Not at all.

Just like any other marketer, in your marketing presentation:

- You have to get people's attention (headline);

- Your offer must make a clear and believable case for your product or service (the story);

- You have to demonstrate, not just tell, what your buyers will have after they use your product or service (benefits);

- Your numbers must be both credible and affordable (pricing);

- Your customers must trust that they will get what you say they will (promise); and

- Your customers must feel safe so they can take the action you want them to take (guarantee).

Soft sell marketing requires the emotional connection and logical credibility that will convince someone that what you have is what they are looking for and that it will work for them.

Don't assume that soft means weak or that soft means you have to disappear yourself. You just have to present your case in a way that's inclusive, respectful, and that ranks the well-being of your customer or potential customer as highly as you rank the fulfillment of your own needs.

Keys to Soft Sell Marketing

At its essence, soft sell marketing:

- Speaks from the seller's heart to the heart-felt needs of the buyer, because the relationship is at the center of the transaction—which is the foundation for creating a long-term customer;

- Honors the buyer's needs as the source of the deepest urgency possible, rather than manufacturing an illusory need in order to ratchet up the drive to buy;

- Relies on the truth to set free the buyer's decision to purchase, and it's in the buyer's felt sense of freedom that trust is created;

- Emphasizes the conscious care and respect the seller has for the potential buyer leading to a marketing process based in conscience and credibility;

- Avoids exaggerated claims, huge promises, and combative language like "explosive" or "crush the competition," because soft sell marketing is about the reality that we are all connected and interdependent— that is, we need each other—and, as we've said, a successful sale is a co-creation between the seller and buyer for the well-being of both.

Some may say that this last point is already a staple in the process of traditional marketing. But if the principle intent of traditional marketing is the accumulation of money, then considering the well-being of the customer is only a tactic not a core purpose.

So Many Are Grateful

Finally, we want to share with you that many soft sell men and women we've spoken with, whether marketers or consumers, are thrilled to be approached in a way that • respects their sensibilities, • speaks to their intelligence, and • acknowledges their ability and desire to discern for themselves what they will buy.

They've told us again and again, and continue to do so, how gratified they are not to feel hammered by over-the-top sales copy, not to be threatened by false claims of limited supply, and not be at the mercy of wild Internet stories of huge fortunes made overnight.

Remember that the vast majority of buyers on and offline are looking for products that fall well within the definition of soft sell, whether it's relationship advice or weight loss, artichokes or fine art. So, in fact, we, as soft sell marketers, are in the mainstream of marketplace wants and needs.

#35. What resources for copywriters do you have that can assist with heart-based web copy?

Because heart-based, soft sell marketing is a relatively new marketing phenomenon, spawned largely on the Internet, there are few copywriting resources we can point to other than our own "Soft Topic Copywriting Secrets" course.

However, there are quite a few men and women practicing conscious marketing and they may (or may not) write their own copy. But again, they don't offer copywriting training—at least not to our knowledge.

A Learning Technique

You can study the work of soft sell writers by practicing this technique.

Google the following keywords:

- conscious copywriting

- heart based copywriting (and heart-based copywriting)

- soft sell copywriting

- heart centered copywriting (and heart-centered copywriting)

When the results appear click the links on the first page of Google's organic search results (the column on the left side of the page). Study what these copywriters have done to achieve a first page position on Google. Begin to get a feel for soft sell copywriting. When you find a sales page that moves you, study it in its entirety.

- Read it aloud to hear the conversational style.

- Write it out by hand, word for word, to absorb it into your psyche.

- Look to understand and feel the connection through the words. As we've emphasized throughout this book, the emotional connection is most important.

Should you find a writing style you like, contact the site owner. Find out who the writer is and make contact. Commit to the study of copywriting as a part of your ongoing business life.

Soft Topic Copywriting Secrets

As we mentioned, we provide a soft sell copywriting course called "Soft Topic Copywriting Secrets." It's a home study course. Our course is designed and dedicated to show service providers and care-givers how to best get their message across from a heart-based perspective.

We ask, do you want to:

- Grab the attention of your readers and still remain credible?

- Get your message across without being pushy?

- Make a sincere promise that does not violate your integrity?

- Appeal to a sense of urgency without hype and phoney gimmicks?

- Inspire your customers to take the action you want them to take and you know they need to take?

We assure you that you can get through all the marketing noise and inspire your readers to listen to you. It's all in how you tell your story— your personal story and the story of your product or service.

Benefits of Soft Topic Copywriting Secrets

Here are just six of the twenty-four benefits our students enjoy that we list in promoting the course:

- Transform the non-tangible benefits of your products and services into clear, concrete, credible images that reach right into your customer's mind and heart;

- Identify the core of your offer, understand it inside and out, and position yourself in your market to be clearly identifiable to those who are looking for you;

- Unearth the specific emotional needs of your readers without guessing, even if you've never done any formal market research;

- Trust your copy to create your customer's trust;

- Avoid over-promising without under-valuing your message as you portray in words the true worth of who you are and what you offer;

- Stop from falling into the most deadly trap of all soft sell traps—copy that's trite or overly sentimental.

Study these bullet points. There are at least two very powerful copywriting techniques you can learn within them as well as absorbing and learning from the tone and feel of the writing.

#36. What resources for copywriters do you have that can assist with heart-based web copy?

The issue of money is central to many soft sell marketers we've spoken with. Why? Because, as we've said, the majority of soft sell, care-oriented marketers don't come from and don't live within a business mindset—us included.

If we did, we'd understand that, although spelled differently, business and $$$$ mean the same thing. They are synonymous. Business is fundamentally, and intentionally about making money—as much money as possible.

But that's not the psychological or spiritual objective of most care-givers. We aren't driven by money—not as our dominant motive. We have to have it, and would love to have enough to live whatever each of us considers very comfortably. But a drive to make money, and more and more money, is not part of the character of most soft sell marketers.

The Pressures of Money

Take a look at some of the negative pressures of money in our culture:

- Money is effectively if not blatantly worshiped;

- The power of money often leads to control and abuse;

- The corruptibility of money creates more and more greed for more and more money.

Just a few distortions that give financial accumulation a bad name. On the other hand, soft sell marketers, by dint of being care-givers, are predisposed to a spiritual orientation. Our primary intention is to create a connection that advances the experience of well-being—for both the seller and the buyer. The payoff is fundamentally and largely emotional—person-to-person, heart-to-heart.

For hard sell marketers, their drive is primarily and exclusively money. It's unimaginable for them to view marketing and selling in any other way.

Is More Better?

Unless you change how you understand and relate to money, the idea of more money for you is moot. You may fantasize about more but you won't manifest more. The "more" question is relevant only to someone for whom money is a driving priority.

A better question for you is—What is the spiritual significance of money? What is in the nature or character of money that it contributes to the physical, psychological, and spiritual enhancement for all parties involved?

Your Soul's Intentions

Like our questioner, you may wrestle with whether or not making more money may be out of integrity with soft sell marketing. But let's look at money in a different way. Let's take it out of a "who-wins/who-loses" competitive context and understand it within a co-creative, collaborative, partnership.

Money is communication, a transfer of energy, a medium for connection, a sign of gratitude. Rather than seeing money as a measure—a quantity—money can be seen as an expression of manifestation—a quality—a signal of soul-based excellence. It reveals the character of someone's internal dimensions as the internal dimensions are revealed in the external world.

Money represents the excellence of character and intention in the co-creation between the seller and buyer of a successful transaction. In this way money expresses a deep, internal richness. More money means not just that you make more sales, it means that the results you promised have been delivered and enjoyed and your customers are both returning to buy from you again and again as well as spreading the word.

Then it's not just about financial accumulation, is it? It's about true, real-world effectiveness. It's a shift in perspective without abandoning the externality of money. That's how money becomes the proof of power—not the power of money but the personal and professional power you manifest through the promise and payoff of your products and services.

Money also represents freedom. Freedom for you, to be sure. But freedom for your customers as well. Freedom from the burden of whatever problem(s) they were saddled with. The more money you earn the more your bottom line represents the freedom you have been able to deliver to your customers—a freedom from concern that money actually does buy.

And what if more money grants you security so that you can keep venturing into manifestation—exploring, discovering, innovating, and bringing to the world your particular genius, assisting those who need the fruits of your creative production?

Is more better? Definitely. And it's particularly satisfying when you align your soul's intentions with your efforts to make the type of commercial connections that lead not only to a better marketplace, but to a better world.

#37. If there was one key thought to maintain while preparing soft sell marketing, what would you suggest that be?

At the core of soft sell marketing, what sets it apart from hard sell is the way we view our customers.

In hard sell marketing the customer is viewed as someone to be maneuvered into buying, someone whose credit card is more the point. Benefits are important but only in the context of closing the sale. Therefore, whatever it takes to grab the potential buyer's interest and keep it long enough to make the sale, so be it.

As a soft sell marketer, the key value to maintain—the key awareness— while preparing your marketing plan, your sales copy, and your customer care is that you and your customer are one and the same:

- In the practical sense of having been burdened with the same problem or problems for which you are providing a solution; and

- In the spiritual sense that you are deeply connected and interdependent—partners in the co-creation of every sale.

When you're aware that your customer is little different from you— and, in a very real sense is you—you'll approach your buyer as someone who:

- Stands in their own dignity;

- Is capable of making self-benefitting decisions with the right guidance; and

- Actually needs what you provide.

No need to brow-beat. No need to harangue and threaten. And no interest in people buying just to stuff money into your bank account.

While it may take a bit longer for you to achieve the substantial returns that are available online and offline, your customer's and your own soul will thank you. Because you are genuinely invested in the co-creative partnership between you—with yours and your buyer's benefit at heart.

This perception of your customer is the core principle and practice that will keep you on the caring and respectful heart-track throughout your marketing plans and implementation.

#38. What is the best way to market a spiritually motivated product?

We characterize a spiritually motivated product as anything that advances consciousness. It's more than just a vehicle for a financial transaction. It enhances and expands the life of both the buyer and the seller, serving as the basis for a partnership between them.

So there are many products that come to market based on a spiritually motivated intention that illuminate and express the deep interdependence at the heart of our being alive on this planet. The spirituality resides in the product producer and is expressed in what he or she offers the world.

The gifts the seller brings to the market are recognized and respected. The needs the buyer brings to the market are recognized and respected. The deepest value each brings, even beyond the need the product satisfies and the profit made, is the connection they create together as they serve themselves by taking real care of each other. That conscious reciprocity is the fundamental transaction. The product/sale is the external conduit for the internal connection.

Now, Specific to Spiritual Products . . .

When it comes to spiritually-oriented products and services, marketing can seem awkward if not downright uncomfortable. Why? Because, when it comes to so-called spiritual products, what most people think of is the palm reader's sign in the basement window or the guy in a weird outfit at the Halloween Faire who guarantees that he will catch any and every ghost in your house. And that doesn't make your perfectly legitimate offer and your sincere intention to help any easier to bring to market.

Yet, more and more people are curious about the powers and mysteries that exist in the unseen. People will pay for products and services that speak to everything from The Law of Attraction to the healing power of prayer, intuitive readings to angelic intervention, and much, much more.

So marketing your spiritually derived and dedicated services and products is no less important than marketing more traditional programs.

A Note of Caution

Paradoxically our note is: Do *not* be cautious in your use of spiritually-oriented language.

If your product or service addresses, for example: Metaphysics, The Prophecies, Energy Healing, The Great Mysteries, Meditation, Kabbalah, Yoga, or any of hundreds or perhaps thousands of other such spiritually motivated programs that could be deemed "far out" in one way or another---do *not* back away.

Stand firm in your commitment to make certain that those who are looking for you will have no problem finding you and understanding the specific product or service you provide.

So, Then . . .

- Make sure to speak to your prospective buyer in the language they most easily understand.

- Don't leave room for guessing or running to the dictionary.

- Put your belief and your confidence out there, center stage, when you deliver your offer and your promise.

- Be sure to put your message where your key audience members will see you. Only you will know, for example, where it would be best to purchase blog ads, or in which kinds of forums you'll want to interact in order to help get out the word.

Whatever you do, do *not* water down or hide what you provide.

#39. What are the pitfalls of soft sell marketing?

Nothing is without obstacle or drawback. And the same is true for soft sell marketing. So we want to share the major challenges we've observed for soft sell marketers.

Sentimentality

Because most soft sell marketers rank high in empathy, and because they lack business training as well as direct and persuasive copywriting skills, they can fall into the trap of sentimentality—over-identifying with the emotionality of their customers and clients.

As a result their sales messages can become sympathetic rather than hopeful, problem-driven rather than solution focused. When this happens the soft sell marketer has lost sight of the rational side of their marketing presentation and the appropriate role of persuasion—a serious loss for both seller and buyer.

Giving Themselves Away

In a marketplace accustomed to both sides operating from an every-man-for-himself ethic, the soft sell marketers' lack of business training complicated by their empathic character structure often leads to under-pricing their products and services. It's not uncommon for soft sell marketers to then feel taken advantage of—even by their own character structure.

In short, soft sell marketers all too often give themselves away. We've done it and know many others who have as well.

Insecure Against Hard Sell

The soft sell marketing orientation is cooperative rather than competitive. Consequently soft sell marketers measure their success primarily by the well-being of their customers rather than the self-focused accumulation of money. While that's a form of spiritual excellence, in our highly competitive, survival-of-the-fittest culture a preference for cooperation carries with it a sometimes conscious, but most often unconscious psychological drag—in other words, a shadow of self-doubt and insecurity.

Blocked in their ability to present their products with clarity and strength, unable to stand out from the crowd and claim their rightful success in the marketplace, the soft sell marketer's self-doubt and insecurity leads to poor marketing and negligible marketing results.

Allergic to Persuasion

For many soft sell, heart-based marketers any form of persuasion seems manipulative and disrespectful—just another form of hype.

> **Judith:** During our promotional tour for our third book *Be Loved for Who You Really Are*, we were in Toronto, very pleased to have booked appearances on every television show in the city including Canada AM, the Canadian equivalent of the "The Today Show" or "Good Morning America."
>
> Nevertheless, one night at dinner I began to cry. I kept saying that " I want our book to sell because it's excellent and can actually help people, not because we have to promote it over and over again. It all seems like hype. Just hype. More and more hype."
>
> Jim was very gentle with me and as we continued talking I realized that I was caught in my father's total lack of respect for the idea and practice of selling. He was an artist who ended up making his living as a car salesman. He hated selling but was very good at it. So his life was tormented

by his own lack of self-respect. As a child I vowed I would never be like him. Yet there I was out promoting our book. How different was I, really?

Well, I've since come to practice selling as a spiritual service. And I know that when done with consciousness and conscience, with a genuine care and consideration for the well-being of our customers and ourselves, selling is not only necessary, it can be an open-hearted, generous, honorable, and profitable career.

I'm sharing my Toronto meltdown-moment to offer comfort if you're struggling with your own "allergic" reaction to the art of persuasion known as marketing.

That's Why We Produce . . .

- "Bridging Heart and Marketing" our Internet marketing conferences where the underlying theme is Selling Is Spiritual Service. (http://www.bridgingheartandmarketing.com)

    During the conference we had several life-changing experiences. The one that impacted our lives the most was the realization that fear was holding us back. Now, most of us have a small sense of that knowledge somewhere in us. But, in one of Judith and Jim's sessions, it resonated in us so deeply that it ignited a fire in us that changed our lives forever. We're now running not only one but (soon) three internet businesses and living the life we had always envisioned.

    Dawn and Tina Jo Stephens, Baja, Mexico

- "Soft Sell Marketers Association" where we provide ongoing training and connections to support soft sell marketers in making their businesses as successful as they want them to be. (http://www.softsellmarketersassociation.org)

Your Soft Sell Marketers Association is brilliant. It's a joy. I wish I'd had this kind of professional association when I got started in marketing.

Art Klein, Catskill, NY

- "Soft Topic Copywriting Secrets" home study course, the only copywriting course for soft sell marketers.
  (http://www.softtopiccopywritingsecrets.com)

  Never knew how off-target I was in my sales copy until I took this course. I learned more about copywriting for my market in just the first couple of sessions than all those years studying with some of the Internet Gurus.

  MaryJo Wagner, PhD, Marble, Colorado

- "Overcoming the Fear of Being Fabulous" our 12-CD program supports men and women to break through to new freedom and success by digging deep into what holds them back.
  (http://www.overcomingthefearofbeingfabulous.com)

  Judith and Jim's questions took me right down to some core issues and the intensity of the process did get me to a breakthrough. You have to be ready, but if you are Judith and Jim will take you there.

  Sonali Chapron, Co-Founder, Beyond Business For Women, Reno, NV

- "Magnify Your Excellence" our 3-day experiential intensive is dedicated to helping participants let their excellence shine through in every area of their lives.
  (http://www.magnifyyourexcellence.com)

WOW! Although our conversation took a direction neither of us had anticipated, we accomplished an incredible amount in a very short time! Thank you so much for your insights, powerful questions, and knowledge. I am so appreciative of your time and energy - and concrete suggestions! Right now I feel at least 10 years lighter -- my shoulders are relaxing -- my head is held higher and I'm smiling just for the fun of smiling! It's fascinating to me that just a couple of questions - and some gentle nudging - can accomplish so much in such a short time! Again, THANK YOU!

Barbara Legan, Sedona, AZ

#40. What information is the most important about myself and my services that I need to share with my potential customers when I promote my services?

As we said in answer to Question #33, your story is one of the most powerful persuaders in your marketing repertoire. Review the questions we listed in the "Assess Your Story" segment of Question #33. Your answers will establish the bottom line message of who you are and what you offer.

To help you with this we want to introduce the idea of your USP— Unique Selling Proposition—which we prefer to call your PSP— Personal Selling Proposition—a marketing technique that will shape and condense your story.

But first we have to ask the question . . .

What Is Your USP?

"USP" stands for Inique Selling Proposition or Unique Selling Position, a term well known in the traditional marketing community. It's a short, direct statement that describes what you do and what your customer can expect from you.

For example, for our "Soft Topic Copywriting Secrets" course we use— Matching Your Message to the Heart of Your Market.

For our "Bridging Heart and Marketing" conferences we use—Selling Is Spiritual Service: Marketing in Alignment with Your Heart-Based Professional Values and Personal Integrity.

For our Soft Sell Marketers Association we use—Where Success and Spirituality Join Together for the Benefit of All.

Why PSP?

Rather than USP, we prefer the phrase Personal Selling Proposition—PSP—because it's more in alignment with our soft sell approach. Most products and services are not all that unique. But everything is personal—deeply personal.

Once you arrive at your PSP, it serves as the source from which the rest of your marketing communications follow.

The Power of Your PSP

Even though every PSP should be concise, we're going to show you just how powerful it is in delivering information.

1) Your PSP is an identifying statement. It's like your name. When your customers see or hear it they know where they are and whether or not they're in the right place.

2) Your PSP differentiates you from others in your market segment. It's usually said that a USP differentiates you from your competition. But when done well, your PSP eliminates the idea of competition, because only you can do what you do in the way that you do it.

3) Your PSP offers your promise—something will occur that results from what you provide. A definable outcome is established.

4) Your PSP sets up an expectation in the mind of your customer. In our copywriting course we teach techniques that show you how to take your message and craft it in such a way that it touches the heart of your prospective customer.

5) Your PSP is a form of giving your word. We must prove that, when you become a member of our Soft Sell Marketers Association, we will do everything we can to assure that spiritual principles and success principles are joined to produce a very specific kind of marketing approach.

6) Your PSP instructs you as to what you have to do to make good on your promise. We—Judith & Jim—are guided by our commitment to creating an alignment between marketing tools and techniques and the personal integrity soft sell marketers insist on when we put together each of our Bridging Heart and Marketing conferences.

7) Your PSP identifies what gap in the market you are filling, what problem you are solving. It expresses your specific point of identification for those who are looking for you. Prior to our Bridging Heart and Marketing conference there were no Internet conferences for the soft sell, service provider community. That is the gap we are filling.

8) Ideally your PSP must be dynamic—it has movement in that it begins somewhere and suggests an end result. It expresses action. And it must be feeling-filled—suggesting not only the quality of what will happen in the now, but the quality of feeling to be expected in the future.

You have much information to share with your prospective customers, and you will, as they become more familiar with who you are and what you do. It all derives from your personal story and the story of your product.

The purpose of working to envision and express your PSP is to achieve specificity and clarity in such a way that you are immediately recognizable and identifiable.

#41. How do you measure the success of soft sell marketing?

When evaluating the success of your soft sell marketing, don't assume that soft sell marketing is something so different that accepted external measures can't apply. They do. And, in addition, we add internal measures.

Traditional External Measures

Business is simple. It's about getting customers and keeping them. The rest is detail.

Following this simple yet elegant maxim, whether you practice soft or hard sell, the top two external measures are traffic and conversion.

Traffic simply means the number of visitors to your website or your brick and mortar store. You must have a continual flow of potential customers to keep your business alive and vital. Without traffic you have no business.

Conversion is the percentage of visitors who purchase your products or services and become customers—converting them from potential to actual customers.

Success can be measured by an increase in traffic and a subsequent increase in paying customers. This means, of course, an increase in your gross income and hopefully in your net profit.

And More . . .

List Building is another necessary element of your success. Online and off your fortune is in your customer list or database—the size of your list and the willingness of your list members to buy. That's why list building is necessarily an ongoing practice.

Recurring Sales is a measure of the results your customers enjoy from what you provide and the trust you've earned with them.

Customer Service—responsive and caring—is the cornerstone of a long-term, commercial relationship and the solid base of your business. Good customer service is evidence of your sincerity and your good business practice.

The external measures of traffic, conversion, list size and loyalty, recurring sales, and income are used for any type of business on or offline.

Internal Soft Sell Measures

Because the external measures are largely, if not exclusively about numbers, you can perform your testing and tracking without contacting your customer base.

On the other hand, the internal measures are largely interactive and require you to get feedback from your list-members—customers and potential customers alike—and/or mastermind group members or other trusted colleagues. In other words, you'll need outside input to find out how well you are doing.

Here are four principle internal measures you can use to keep yourself on track and on point.

Authenticity – Does what you promise measure up with what your product actually delivers? Does your product walk your talk?

When you and your product walk your talk, your customers can confidently expect to achieve the results you claim your product will deliver. And what have you done? You've established a believable expectation—and that's one of the measures of authenticity.

Your words and your products are genuine. Real. Free from deceit, falseness, or exaggeration. They are what they appear to be. What you say and what your product can do come from a reliable source—you. In other words, you can be believed.

Transparency – Technically "transparency" is defined as – having the property of allowing visibility so that bodies situated beyond or behind can be distinctly seen."

When it comes to sales, transparency means the motives and real intent of the seller are revealed and available permitting the buyer to make a secure judgment. In short, the buyer can trust that he or she is not being fooled.

In dollars and cents terms, transparency insures (or at least attempts to insure) that the sale goes through and there won't be a request for a refund.

Interdependence – "When we try to pick out anything by itself, we find it hitched to everything else in the Universe." John Muir

How more clearly and elegantly can the fact of our interdependence, our interconnectedness, our mutual need of one another be expressed? Interdependence is the foundation upon which soft sell marketing stands—because we all exist within the interdependent nature of being alive in this universe. Nothing stands alone. Life *is* relationship.

How does your awareness of the interdependence of all of life impact your marketing efforts?

How do you perceive your customer in the context of the interconnectedness which is the stamp of life?

Integrity – A soft sell transaction includes a serious and sincere regard for consequences. It's not just about getting products out the door, but also about the impact of those products on the long-term well-being of customers.

In a soft sell transaction there is a wholeness that includes awareness of the other. Buyer and seller regard each other—not as objects to be manipulated or defended against—but as the other member of the partnership.

The integrity of a soft sell transaction emerges from the appreciation both parties give to the value of their relationship—a value based on mutual necessity and mutual benefit.

This soft sell, heart-based partnership model isn't just window dressing. It's the foundation for the success of your sales and your ongoing business—marketing and selling with consciousness and conscience.

#42. What are the key understandings for staying in "both and" balance?

We appreciate this question because it allows us to speak to the balance of the both-and perspective compared with an either-or perspective. The latter is exclusionary, insisting that the result must be one or the other—but not both.

The both-and perspective is inclusionary implying the possibility of a result produced by the co-creative interaction of both sides of a transaction which otherwise could not have been produced by either side alone.

The both-and point of view as an operating principle can prevent the abuse of greed while setting up the basis for healthy long-term customer relationships.

The fact is, we are all co-creative partners whether we're conscious of that fact or not. What's even more basic than how we function is the fact that we are, every minute of every day, in relationship. This fact is incontrovertible. To believe otherwise is not only an illusion, it's an illusion that breeds a form of insanity—as exposed by the greed and collapse we recently witnessed on Wall Street and the unraveling of the sub-prime mortgage market (Fall, 2008).

The Insanity of Separation

And then there was the Enron scandal of 2001. Remember that? The management of the Enron corporation had been operating with the conscious intent of gouging as much as possible in fees out of the State of California Power Authority. Their insanity was not only expressed by their malevolent intent to accumulate monies far beyond what was appropriate, but in their lack of care about the hardship and injury they knew they would bring upon the consumers in California.

Their deepest insanity was the degree of separation they felt—emotionally and communally—such that they even believed they would not be harmed by what they were doing, nor would the employees of Enron.

This was not just legal jeopardy which ultimately resulted in their imprisonment. But their insanity ignored the psychological, moral, and spiritual damage they would bring upon themselves and the financial ruin they foisted upon the many who trusted them.

To say it another way, they had no sense of a social contract. So they betrayed and violated themselves, everyone else involved, and the basic interdependence of life—the connectedness that houses the sacred.

Within Enron there was no both-and balance. There was such excess as to virtually eradicate any sense of balance whatsoever.

The Enron executives are a vivid example of the loss of connection with the community in which they lived—not just their local Texas community but the community of humanity, the community of existence.

The idea and belief in the separate, stand-alone individual, and the pedestal onto which that belief has been elevated in our society, creates the context for the maladaptive and malevolent commercial and personal results that occur every day. Enron just happens to be an egregious and very dramatic instance of it.

The Sanity of Soft Sell and Both-And Balance

Soft sell marketing is all about both-and balance. When we live with awareness of this balance, our awareness of the undeniable connection between one and all is the basis for our appreciation of the inherent value of both—*both* the seller *and* the buyer—as a co-creative team. This awareness makes it nearly impossible to ignore or deny the impact of our beliefs and behaviors on the rest of the human community.

Seventeenth century philosopher Immanuel Kant developed what he called the "categorical imperative" asking us all to consider our actions by the following standard. We paraphrase:

> Would you do what you're about to do if you knew that your action would be elevated to a universal law for all others to follow?

From a soft sell perspective this question points to the extent that our behavior impacts others. For example—would you continue to exaggerate your claims and promotional promises if you knew that your exaggeration would be elevated to a universal law for everyone to follow? Can you see how your behavior would come back to injure you?

Don't be deceived by the argument that your personal or professional choices are not elevated to universal law. It's true, technically they're not. But, the fact is, the reach of your impact extends far beyond what you can perceive.

And, to bring this idea closer to home, would you teach your children to exaggerate? Or do you want your children to be misled by the exaggerations of others?

So How to Stay In Balance?

To stay in both-and balance as a soft sell marketer:

- You want to be sure that the benefits accruing from your offer support the intentions of both you and your customer as equally as you can make that happen;

- When your transaction is based in both-and, you will experience a sense of poise and emotional elegance—not just graceful but grace-filled;

- You will manifest emotional stability and comfort because your offer will be grounded in the truth of the whole rather than in the combat of me-first competition;

- Interdependence, cooperation, and partnership will be evident in feeling and consciousness, defusing your ego demands and relegating them to a non-dominant status;

- You can trust your choices because your conscience is leading you to right-action;

- All of the elements of your transaction, from the initial promotion to the opening of the relationship with your customer, are functioning in harmony, and that harmony breeds success; and

- When you are in harmony you will have integrated the well-being of both you and your customer. You will create and produce a result that will be both beautiful and beneficial—both a pleasure and a profit for *both* you *and* your customer.

#43. Is customer follow-up important in making long lasting relationships?

There may be nothing more important to the robust health of any business than the loyalty of long-lasting customers. They've purchased from you. They like your products and/or services. They believe in you. And they're more than likely to buy from you again and again. And they'll tell their friends.

We have to admit that keeping focused on cultivating lasting relationships with our list members and customers has been a bit of a challenge for us.

We come from the world of psychotherapy—40 years combined in a profession that makes connection with your clients outside the consulting room unethical and possibly illegal. Connection in the consulting room is important to the therapeutic process, but it's governed by the need for the therapist to remain in observer mode so that the relationship remains professional rather than personal.

We also both come from families that didn't connect well, even with other family members much less neighbors and work associates. So we deeply appreciate that the world of marketing is the perfect vehicle to continually remind us to step into a closer connection with our list members, everyone who attends our events, and the members of our Soft Sell Marketers Association.

If this challenge resonates with you as well, we encourage you to join in allowing the need for follow up and ongoing connection to spur you to grow your business as you grow your Self.

The 80-20 Rule

Assuming your products and services provide good, important value to your customers, research has shown that approximately 20% of your customers want to have a long standing, mutually respectful and collaborative relationship with you. They want to give you their appreciation and be thanked in return. They want to take your surveys and feel that their opinions are valued. They want to get special offers from time to time, whether for your list members only, or for customers only.

While you want to stay as connected as possible, the other 80% of your list members may or may not ever buy from you, much less buy from you again. So they're not likely to become members of your core community. As you may have heard, 80% of your business will come from 20% of your list. So be sure to value and honor your 20%!

How Do You Want to Be Treated?

Take a moment and think about when you're a customer. How do you want to be treated?

We imagine that when you make a purchase you want to be thanked, right? So your follow-up Thank You note needs to start immediately—on your online Thank You Page—and offline perhaps in the form of a Thank You card.

Your buyers would like to hear from you that you care about their using and benefitting from your product. So you can use an online autoresponder message, scheduling it to come a few days after they've had a chance to experience at least a bit of what they ordered, asking them how they are benefitting from your product.

Perhaps they'd like to receive follow up messages several times, particularly if your messages are giving them tips and hints for maximizing the benefits of the product or service they bought.

As the seller, you might want to hold a Q & A call every so often, allowing for person-to-person connection and opening the way to put to rest any confusion or unmet needs about your product or service.

And pretty soon, it's going to be time to think about what else you can provide for your customers that will add value to their lives and continue to build the closer connection between you.

An Even Closer Connection

What do you have to offer? Take an inventory of your products and/or services as well as your untapped skills and talents. Because this is a marvelous opportunity to create a new program based on what you know your current and future customers want or need.

As you continue through this process, remember that as the seller, it's your job to stay in touch with your buyers. This way you create mutually beneficial relationships that help all of you grow in whatever ways fit with your areas of expertise. At the same time you tap into the spiritual connection made available by the relationships you share even though, on the Internet, you'll never meet in person and may be continents apart.

> **Judith:** Appreciative feedback from our customers, affiliates and colleagues, and our SSMA members usually makes me teary, touching my heart and renewing my vow to make sure soft sell marketers don't have to struggle like we did when we first entered the world of sales and marketing.

> **Jim:** I treasure the insight, the spiritual wisdom our community members grace us with, reminding me that I am not nearly as alone as I've felt all my life (despite the magic of Judith's and my more than 20-year marriage). So we live in deep gratitude for the long lasting relationships with our list members, customers, and SSMA members, just as they tell us is the case for them.

Commit to following up with your customers and list members in as many ways as feels right for you. In this way the heart of soft sell marketing is made real in your everyday life and that of your customers, and you experience even more deeply the benefits of having a soul-based business.

#44. What's one thing I definitely need to do to successfully sell in a soft sell manner?

This is not so much a "to do" as a "to be." In order to tap into the powerful core of soft sell marketing you must approach what you are doing with love:

- Love for the people you are serving because they are your partners;

- Love for their needs;

- Love for your product or service;

- Love for the benefits you provide through your product or service; and

- Love for your self as you partner in co-creating sales with your customers.

When your marketing is infused with love, you not only stay far away from any danger of selling out—either you or your customers—you tap into a reservoir of clear energy, magnetic energy, an energy of cosmic persuasion that you cannot reach any other way, and that your customers can't help but find appealing.

Love your customers and they will love you back.

Love and Marketing

Until the introduction of soft sell marketing, the primary if not exclusive point of marketing campaigns has been to increase the bottom line.

Too often, on the Internet, the product was flawed, and even inadequate to the benefits suggested by the promotion. From a marketing point of view the well-being of the customer was largely incidental—short of damage that could result in bad word of mouth or even a lawsuit.

But now as you market with consciousness and conscience, you are alert to rank your customers' well-being as just as important as your own. In doing this, your key objective is to include your care for your customers—and that's called love.

It's not romantic love. It's not the love you feel for your family. But it is a dimensional love:

- A form of self-love when you identify with your potential customer and you can see how you would want to be treated;

- Love of your potential or actual customer as you market to them with care and respect, authenticity and transparency.

So the heartbeat of soft sell marketing is love.

Now What to Do

1) How often do you express to your potential customers your authentic and transparent passion for what you have to offer?

2) How often do you share your excitement about the success stories that come back from your buyers?

3) How often do you reveal the deep calling that brought you to do what you do, so your customers can feel the heart of your commitment to them?

You may not think of sharing your passion, your success stories, and your professional calling as love, but it is. Because, when you do, you show yourself—emotionally and spiritually—and open the truth of who you are, which is the basis of your connection with those who do business with you. And that is love.

We're not getting woo-woo here. Not at all. We're simply calling you to share more of yourself with your buyers, so they can feel who you are, so they can identify with you, so they can feel safe buying from you, and trust that they will get what you say they will get.

It all starts with letting yourself be known.

Practice expressing your care for your buyers and potential customers through your sales copy, through other writing whether articles, special reports or books, through radio and/or television appearances. In other words, in the context of your business, open the window to a new degree of intimacy in your communication.

From Our Hearts to Yours

We trust that, as you've been reading this book, you can feel our love for soft sell marketing. We've openly communicated our care for you and for your customers page after page, suggestion after suggestion.

This book isn't just a platform statement. It's not just a teaching tool. It's our way of sharing an orientation toward sales and marketing that we know benefits you, your readers and customers, and benefits the well being of the entire world through the vehicle of soft sell, heart-based commercial transactions.

So as you express more of your love through the marketing you do to build your business, not only will you increase your sales and help attract more and more list members, it will also feed your soul—day after day after day.

#45. Do you see soft sell marketing as the future trend in developing customer relationships?

Soft sell marketing shows every indication that it is the future trend in developing good, long lasting customer relations.

In fact we recently received a promotional email sent out by internationally recognized copywriter, Bob Bly. He's been writing for years and is very well known in the direct marketing as well as Internet marketing industries.

His many clients include: AARP, CBS Market Watch, Forbes, Harvard Business School, Kiplinger, McGraw-Hill, Nature, Nightingale-Conant, New York Times Syndicate, Prentice Hall, and Scientific American.

Here's what he wrote:

> "The teaching of how to make money marketing information on the Internet has gone from an honorable, honest profession to a hype-filled, slime-infested jungle. Each day, the claims get more and more outrageous.

> 'I made $1 million in 17 seconds on the Internet!' one promoter screams.

> 'Join my Delta Mega Force Team today and get a Rolls Royce with your first affiliate commission check,' another shouts even more loudly.

"Does brag-and-boast advertising like this - especially from so-called marketing gurus you never heard of before make you skeptical?

"To me, these outrageous promotions ... sorely lacking in credibility ... make me want to toss my cookies!"

It's the kind of over-the-top hype Bly writes about that prompted us to start speaking out about soft sell marketing, because traditional hard sell Internet marketing has become, in many cases, ever more outrageous. Hype-filled. Not credible.

When genuine, heartfelt emotion is absent, copywriters are compelled to use hype which pushes their sales message over the top. They're forced to try to generate a feeling response from their readers, but they only have their own brain-space to work with.

We welcome Bly's acknowledgment of the problem for which soft sell marketing is the solution.

The Future of Marketing

And as for the future of marketing, Jim came across an article about a new book *The Way We'll Be*, written by conservative pollster John Zogby. He's a political right of center opinion taker and we point that out, not for political reasons, but to highlight the fact that what he writes about in his book would not automatically be expected from a man of his political leanings.

Zogby is a very credible and honest pollster and that's what makes his findings so remarkable—and so relevant to the continued rise of soft sell marketing, online and off.

The generation now coming of age Zogby calls the "New Globals." Quoting Zogby, he defines them as "that group of Americans, between ages 18 and 29, who:

- Focus on relationships;

- Are the first color-blind Americans;

- Possess a global perspective;

- Want honesty and fairness;

- Appeal to the best in humanity, not the worst;

- Consider themselves citizens of the planet; and

- Demand authenticity and not spin. They yearn for authenticity like no generation before. They've had it up to here with marketing, whether political or commercial, that's all hype and a payoff that falls far short."

The Promise of Soft Sell Marketing

Soft sell marketing is all about authenticity. The seller has authentic care and passion for the product or service being sold. And the buyer sincerely values being cared for through the solution to their need. It is much like a beautiful dance.

When done well, soft sell marketing *is* the dance of life lived out on the stage of commercial exchange. The giving and the taking are equally fine expressions of all that it means to be human. And the needs on both sides of the exchange never end. They remain with us, each and every day. Year after year.

So as we continue to open our relationship with you, dear committed reader, we thank you for your authentic interest in what we've had to say. Because it is true that soft sell marketing is the future trend in marketing and sales, and in developing long lasting customer relations.

By reading this book, you are our customer. And we look forward to when we may meet again, and developing a very long lasting relationship with you.

As we say: **Soft Sell Is Not a Revolution. It's an Evolution.**

Ah, what a lovely dance!

Join the Soft Sell Marketers Association (SSMA)
Where Success and Spirituality Join Together for the Benefit of All

Where You Will Be:

- Welcomed and valued for who you are—Beginner–Been at it a while–Advanced Internet Marketer;

- Recognized for where you are and what you need to grow your business;

- Encouraged to follow the freedom of your creative vision so you can;

Speed up your learning	Build your confidence
Trust your passion to excel	Expand your influence
Create the success of your dreams	And help heal the world

Soft Sell Marketers Association—Your Online Home

Judith and Jim's weekly calls are so addictive I have to listen even though it's one of my busiest times. Now I'm learning to Tweet and Twitter and do Facebook in spite of myself, and I'm looking forward to more!

Dr. Susan Lange, Santa Monica, CA, Meridian Holistic Health Center,

www.meridianholistic.com

Thank You for the NEW ways you've shown me to feel good about being in business with this new brand of marketing you call "soft sell." It can be even MORE effective than traditional "hard sell." The best part is what you teach spreads a good vibe to me as a business owner and to my customers.

Jae Jans, Web Producer, SEO Expert, http://JaeJans.com

Our SSMA call, "Internet Marketing as a Spiritual Teacher" showed me the difference between logical and emotional motivation and that I've virtually been trying to produce orange juice from apples. What a revelation! And a spiritual lesson as well. Thank you!

Vicki Lennox, Brisbane, Qld Australia, Emerging Swan Coaching

http://www.EmergingSwanCoaching.com

JOIN AS A GOLD MEMBER NOW
GO TO:

http://www.softsellmarketersassociation.org

Soft Sell Resources Page

(All URLs mentioned in the Book can be found on this page)

As previously mentioned, these Soft Sell Marketing Resources are available to help you market your products and services in alignment with your personal and professional integrity:

NOTE: To make it easy for you we have gathered all of these resources online at http://www.theheartofmarketing.com/resources so that you just have to go to that page and click the links for whatever interests you.

Or

You can type in any of the links below and go directly to whichever resource you want.

➥**Soft Sell Marketers Association** - Where you grow your self as you grow your business

http://www.softsellmarketersassociation.org

➥**Bridging Heart and Marketing** – The first and only soft sell Internet marketing conference

http://www.bridgingheartandmarketing.com

➥**Bridging Heart & Marketing Blog** – Marketing with consciousness and conscience

http://www.bridgingheartandmarketing.com/blog

➥**Overcoming The Fear of Being Fabulous** – Our 12-CD program helps you dig deep into what's been holding you back from greater success and the larger life you desire.

http://www.overcomingthefearofbeingfabulous.com

➥**Magnify Your Excellence** – Our 3-day intensive to help you become the expression of your deepest gifts. Remove the unconscious blocks that hold you back, stand confidently in the world, and contribute to the betterment of the planet and everyone on it.

http://www.magnifyyourexcellence.com

➥**Soft Topic Copywriting Secrets** (home study course) – Match your message to the heart of your market and draw customers to trust you, buy from you again and again and spread the word.

http://www.softtopiccopywritingsecrets.com

➥**How to Build Your Soft Sell Marketing Platform** – Establish your leadership presence in your specific market. Follow our advice in this downloadable audio gift:

http://www.bridgingheartandmarketing.com/platformbonus

➥**The Power and Profit of Soft Sell Marketing** – Make a declaration for the abundance that can be yours as you listen to this downloadable audio gift:

http://tinyurl.com/softsellpowerandprofit

➥**The Art of Testimonials** – Everything you need to know about the best, most effective types of testimonials, and the ethics involved:

http://www.softtopiccopywritingsecrets.com/tat

➥**Ask Database Software Program** – Used to collect the 772 questions that led to this book and highly recommended to survey your list members:

http://www.softsellaskdatabase.com

➥**Teleseminar Secrets** – This is where we started online. Now you can experience Alex Mandossian's Teleseminar Secrets preview call any time you want:

http://www.foryoursoftsellteleseminars.com

➥**First Step Internet Marketing** – The only course for the true beginner.

http://www.firststepinternetmarketing.com

➥**Online Money Magnets** – Tactics, tips, strategies, and secrets for making money online.

http://www.onlinemoneymagnets.com

➥**You Are A Miracle** – There has never been nor will there ever be another you. Get your "miracle" screen saver to remind you.

http://www.youareamiracle.net

➥**How Do You Know Your Soul Calling** – Find out how to listen to what your soul-based business wants from and for you:

http://www.judithandjim.com/soulcalling

YOUR FREE

BONUS

During our first Bridging Heart and Marketing Internet marketing conference we delivered the keynote address titled:

Selling Is Spiritual Service

A $49.95 Value Absolutely Free

Just Go To:
http://www.theheartofmarketing.com/spiritualservice
And download our special gift to you — the video of our keynote presentation

Selling Is Spiritual Service

You opened my mind to vast possibilities and my husband and I are now successfully putting many of them into our online business. I want you guys to really know how you changed my life. I have been swamped with good stuff since I've been back from your conference.
Janet Jackson, Los Angeles, CA

What's Your Most Pressing Question About Marketing From The Heart?

Please let us know
We Will Use It To Support Who You Are And What You Want To Do With Your Business

Just Go To:
http://www.theheartofmarketing.com/ask
And Enter Your Most Pressing Question About Marketing From The Heart

And to say Thank You we will give you access to two 60-minute MP3 Audio Downloads

FREE TO YOU

Audio #1 – Tracy Repchuk, Quantum Leap Coach; Janet Beckers, Founder of Wonderful Web Women; and Lou D'Alo, Power Up Coaching

Audio #2 – James Roche, The Product Info Guy; Christina Hills, The Shopping Cart Queen; David Riklan, founder of SelfGrowth.com; Jeff Herring, The Article Marketing Guy; and Renee Piane, International Networking Expert

They were all featured speakers at our Bridging Heart and Marketing II conference in September 2008. We interviewed them about how they use our soft sell approach in their marketing practices and the results they are getting in their businesses.

Thank you in advance for sharing your remaining questions about soft sell marketing and marketing from the heart.

Other Books By Judith & Jim

Be Loved for Who You Really Are

This book is a beacon of hope. It will open you to what love wants from you and where love must take you—and it will show you the value in every step along the way.

http://tinyurl.com/dlmfc

Opening to Love 365 Days a Year

A collection of insightful essays and transformative affirmations revealing the daily adventure of true, passionate, lasting love and romance.

http://tinyurl.com/cfbrz

The Smart Couple's Guide to the Wedding of Your Dreams

Your wedding journey—throughout the planning and preparation— can be a time of great romance and joyous fun, and it can help you set the foundation for a truly fabulous marriage.

http://www.tinyurl.com/c8sd8

The New Intimacy

This is a book about love and intimacy. But, more important, it's a book about finding love and intimacy in what you may believe is a very unlikely place—in the differences between you and your partner.

http://tinyurl.com/k9k7f

Living Your Love Every Day eBook

How to keep romance alive from beginning to end. Stories of real romance enjoyed every day.

http://www.judithandjim.com/livingyourlove

Relationship Resources from Judith & Jim

➡**Smart Dating for Success Every Time – Guaranteed!** – Most of what you've been told about dating is wrong, even dangerous, pointing you right at heartbreak. But when you become a smart dater you'll attract only the people who are right for you!

http://www.judithandjim.com/smartdating

➡**Love Made Simple** – Have you mistaken fantasy love for real love? That's painful. Now you can make love simple and make it last forever—when you understand and enjoy the core elements that create real romance and a long lasting, fulfilling relationship.

http://www.judithandjim.com/lovemadesimple/

➡**Keeping Romance Alive and The Promise of Conflict** – Do you want the pleasure of sweet, tender romance . . . the real thing? Not just now and then but every day? Romance can be yours anywhere! Anytime!

http://www.fromdatingtomarriage.com/keepingromancealive

➡**Romantic IQ Community** – If real romance is what you're looking for, you'll be at home with us.

Take our Romantic IQ Quiz. Join and become a premium member.

http://www.romanticiq.com

➡**LoveLifeExpress.com** – The only dating community that shows you how to make every date a success. Get your love life on track when you become a free member today!

http://lovelifeexpress.com

We Acknowledge and Are Grateful to . . .

We wouldn't have written this book if we hadn't experienced a serious, soul-wrenching dilemma when we started marketing online. With no background in sales or business, we entered the world of online marketing totally naive and trusting. So when we were confronted with the almost universal use of hard sell tactics, which we tried to copy, it gave us a serious, life changing wake-up call. It didn't fit with who we are or who we provide service to.

Without this experience we would never have noticed the serious need for a new way of marketing and selling.

Without our dilemma we would never have begun speaking out about the need for soft sell marketing and marketing from the heart.

Without our wake-up call we would never have paid such close attention when we met other soft sell marketers at conferences.

We are deeply grateful to all those who talked with us about their frustration and dissatisfaction with the hard sell tactics and their need for another way, a way that would fit with their values and ideals. And we are grateful that they kept telling us that they could find no other model of marketing that they could follow or learn from.

That's why we dedicate *The Heart of Marketing* to all soft sell marketers, especially those of you who helped us find our voice, who helped us understand that our background in psychology, spirituality, and relationships made us well-grounded to become the leading voice for soft sell marketing.

We're grateful to our many Soft Topic Copywriting Secrets students who expressed their deep appreciation for learning how to use their own soul-based sales voice to promote their expert products and services.

We are deeply grateful to our Bridging Heart and Marketing conference participants, speakers, and sponsors as well as all the members of our Soft Sell Marketers Association for reinforcing our determination to become more and more vocal about the need for a profound change in how commerce is conducted—and not just by soft sell marketers.

And we are indebted to all 772 men and women from all over the world who responded to our AskDatabase survey and asked us their most important questions about soft sell marketing, so that we could answer their most universal concerns in this book.

We want to thank David Hancock for supporting us and helping this book come to life through his Morgan James Publishing house. He's a clear and open-minded listener, adaptable to the many shifts that occur in the book-birthing process, and emotionally very generous. We now consider David a friend and look forward to future projects together.

The marketing expertise contributed by Rick Frishman has been stellar. He knows publicity, promotion, marketing, and the Internet, and he is unbounded in his creativity and helpfulness.

And, as part of our Morgan James family, we thank Heather Kirk for her fine design expertise and talent that brought this book to life in print.

We thank Rachel Lopez for her beautiful book cover. Her intuitive understanding of what we wanted was extraordinary and she expressed it with elegance and meaning.

We also thank Sherry Duke for managing the publication process all the way through.

We owe a special thank you to Jim Howard, also at Morgan James, for giving us our perfect book title and sub-title. For our previous books we've endured what we called "title hell," struggling to find a title that accurately described the book, and at the same time, would speak to the potential reader and be commercially successful.

With Jim's keen sensitivity to who we are and how we feel about soft sell marketing, he gave us the gift of *The Heart of Marketing: Love Your Customers and They Will Love You Back*. We are so pleased and so grateful!

Finally we want to acknowledge, with our appreciation, those people who read the near-final manuscript and gave us their unvarnished feedback which helped us make the kind of last minute changes that clean up little confusions that we, as the writers, are too close to catch: Diane McLain, Jae Jans, Susan and Julian Lange, and JC Shardo.

Because the voice of commerce runs the world, we thank you in advance for joining us in making the world a better place by bridging your heart with your marketing—standing strong in your own integrity while respecting and caring for the integrity of your customers.

About Judith & Jim

Judith Sherven, PhD and Jim Sniechowski, PhD are a husband and wife psychology team. With no background in sales or marketing they've created an expansive online career in less than four years. The leading voice for the soft sell approach to marketing and sales, they are best known for producing the only Internet marketing conference for the soft sell community which they call "Bridging Heart and Marketing."

They also provide their popular "Soft Topic Copywriting Secrets" home study course. And with partner Tom Justin they developed the only course for the true Internet marketing beginner, "First Step Internet Marketing," with students around the world.

They founded the Soft Sell Marketers Association (SSMA) to provide support, training, and community for fellow soft sell marketers. The SSMA is dedicated to helping you grow your business as you grow your Self.

Their approach to marketing focuses on the internal elements of marketing as well as the external. They believe if you don't have a solid internal foundation, your business may succeed but will never be fulfilling.

To assist their colleagues toward that fulfillment, they have produced "Overcoming the Fear of Being Fabulous," a 12-CD program that digs deep into what holds people back, and a weekend intensive they call "Magnify Your Excellence."

Judith & Jim are the bestselling authors of five relationship books. *Be Loved for Who You Really Are* (St. Martin's Press), *The New Intimacy* (HCI), *Opening to Love 365 Days a Year* (HCI), *The Smart Couple's*

Guide to the Wedding of Your Dreams (New World Library), and *Living Your Love Every Day* (eBook).

Judith is a clinical psychologist who worked in private practice for twenty-two years. Jim holds a doctorate in Human Behavior and co-founded the Men's Health Network in Washington, D.C.

They are popular and inspiring international speakers and trainers. As guest experts they've been on over 1500 television and radio shows including Oprah, The View, The O'Reilly Factor, 48 Hours, CNN, Canada AM, and The Daily Buzz.

They've written for or been interviewed by hundreds of publications including the Los Angeles Times, Chicago Tribune, USA Today, the Boston Globe, Wall Street Journal, Cosmo, O, Bridal Guide, Redbook, Ladies Home Journal, Playboy, Essence, Women's Day, Family Circle, Parents, Brides, Men's Health, and Best Life.

Married 21 years, Judith & Jim currently live in Las Vegas.

For more about what Judith & Jim offer, please go to — www.judithandjim.com

BUY A SHARE OF THE FUTURE IN YOUR COMMUNITY

These certificates make great holiday, graduation and birthday gifts that can be personalized with the recipient's name. The cost of one S.H.A.R.E. or one square foot is $54.17. The personalized certificate is suitable for framing and will state the number of shares purchased and the amount of each share, as well as the recipient's name. The home that you participate in "building" will last for many years and will continue to grow in value.

Here is a sample SHARE certificate:

HABITAT FOR HUMANITY

THIS CERTIFIES THAT

YOUR NAME HERE

HAS INVESTED IN A HOME FOR A DESERVING FAMILY

1985-2005

TWENTY YEARS OF BUILDING FUTURES IN OUR COMMUNITY ONE HOME AT A TIME

1200 SQUARE FOOT HOUSE @ $65,000 = $54.17 PER SQUARE FOOT
This certificate represents a tax deductible donation. It has no cash value.

YES, I WOULD LIKE TO HELP!

I support the work that Habitat for Humanity does and I want to be part of the excitement! As a donor, I will receive periodic updates on your construction activities but, more importantly, I know my gift will help a family in our community realize the dream of homeownership. **I would like to SHARE in your efforts against substandard housing in my community!** *(Please print below)*

PLEASE SEND ME _____ SHARES at $54.17 EACH = $ $_____

In Honor Of: _____

Occasion: (Circle One)   HOLIDAY   BIRTHDAY   ANNIVERSARY

      OTHER: _____

Address of Recipient: _____

Gift From: _____ *Donor Address:* _____

Donor Email: _____

I AM ENCLOSING A CHECK FOR $ $_____ PAYABLE TO HABITAT FOR HUMANITY OR PLEASE CHARGE MY VISA OR MASTERCARD *(CIRCLE ONE)*

Card Number _____ Expiration Date: _____

Name as it appears on Credit Card _____ Charge Amount $ _____

Signature _____

Billing Address _____

Telephone # Day _____ Eve _____

PLEASE NOTE: Your contribution is tax-deductible to the fullest extent allowed by law.
Habitat for Humanity • P.O. Box 1443 • Newport News, VA 23601 • 757-596-5553
www.HelpHabitatforHumanity.org